A
JOURNEY
TO A BYGONE
STATE

D1425421

DDRMUSEUMVERLAG

Editor Robert Rückel

Text Andreas Menn, Robert Rückel, Katrin Strohl, Dr. Jochen Voit, Dr. Stefan Wolle

Translation Andrew Smith

Design, typesetting, illustrations Constantin Bänfer

Publisher DDR Museum Verlag GmbH, Karl-Liebknecht-Str. 1, 10178 Berlin

Printed Medialogik, Im Husarenlager 6a, 76187 Karlsruhe

Second Edition, May 2012, Printed in Germany

Acknowledgements Melanie Alperstaedt, Dajana Alschner, Berliner Mauer-Archiv,
Berlinische Galerie, Bezirksmuseum Marzahn-Hellersdorf, Ines Buchmann, Bundesarchiv,
Bundesbeauftragter für die Unterlagen der Staatssicherheit, Marcel Gassner,
Harald Hauswald, Janine Henschel, Albert Hulm, Anke Kaprol, Martin Klötzke, Horst Laurisch,
Elmar Paul, Polizeihistorische Sammlung Berlin, Presse- und Informationsamt der Bundes-
regierung, Berndt Püschel, Michael Richter, Robert-Havemann-Gesellschaft, Gerhard Rückel,
Dieter Schmidt, Stadtarchiv Leipzig, Stiftung Gedenkstätte Berlin-Hohenschönhausen,
Hans-Michael Schulze, Andrew Smith, Jens Stoll, Tina Strauch, Bernhard Wagner, Oliver Wia,
Silvana Wrusch and all our associate staff, donors, museum guides and supporters.

Bibliographic information by the German National Library

The German National Library lists this publication in the German National Bibliography.
Detailed bibliographic data is available on the Internet (http://dnb.ddb.de).

GDR-Guide – A journey to a bygone state
ISBN 978-3-939801-17-7

This publication follows on from ISBN 978-3-939801-14-6 »GDR-Guide – Everyday life
in a long-gone state in 22 chapters« and ISBN 978-3-939801-01-6 »The GDR Museum.
A guide to the permanent exhibition. A hands-on experience of everyday life«

Every effort has been made to verify the accuracy of information provided in this book, but
no warranty can be given and no liability assumed by the editor or the publishing company.

© 2012 DDR Museum Verlag GmbH, Karl-Liebknecht-Str. 1, 10178 Berlin
Phone: (030) 847 123 73 - 0, Fax: (030) 847 123 73 - 9,
Internet: www.ddr-verlag.de, E-Mail: info@ddr-verlag.de

GDR-GUIDE

A
JOURNEY
TO A BYGONE
STATE

Robert Rückel (ed.)

DDRMUSEUM**VERLAG**

A WARM WELCOME

Director Robert Rückel

In an interview given shortly before the opening of the DDR Museum in July 2006, I was asked for my response to the view, widely held by museum curators and historians, that an exhibition focusing on everyday life would serve to play down the GDR's status as a dictatorship. The publication in 2006 of the findings of a report to establish a historical commission to »investigate the SED dictatorship« combined with the opening of our museum sparked a nation-wide debate of this topic. Those who identified the Stasi as the sole defining element of life in East Germany argued that the GDR could only be understood from the perspective of its victims. Any other attempt to write the history of East Germany was driven by »ostaligia«, a yearning to return to the Communist past.

How can seeking a broader perspective on a state be accused of trivialization? The GDR was clearly a dictatorship, which meant that the state (as with all authoritarian regimes) exerted a greater influence on the lives of its citizens than would a democracy. However, this mere fact does not mean that the inhabitants of a dictatorship do not smile, laugh, play, love and disobey. This is the reality of everyday life and as such is an integral part of the history of the GDR.

We have always been interested in past ways of life: Roman toilets, medieval contraception and baroque furniture. Without an awareness of such everyday practices, we will never be able to understand the unique nature of each epoch. The same stands for the GDR – a complete understanding of its nature requires an awareness not just of closed borders and constant surveillance, but shortages, the weekly oath ceremony and full employment.

Only a year after opening its doors, the DDR Museum advanced to become one of the most-visited museums of contemporary history in Germany and one of Berlin's premier historical attractions. Some 500,000 satisfied visitors per year and ten thousand international media reports demonstrated not only the level of popular interest in the everyday realities of the GDR but its importance in understanding Germany's Communist past.

The »Schroeder report« published in 2008 revealed an alarming ignorance amongst German schoolchildren of the GDR and its history. Writing in a newspaper article, Stefan Wolle suggested that the GDR seems to become more attractive with every year that passes. Such findings oblige museums and other agencies of political education to provide an objective account of all aspects of life in the GDR. Only through the juxtaposition of the positive (or supposedly positive) and negative aspects of the Socialist system can we hope to reach an adequate understanding of the German Democratic Republic.

We very much hope that our exhibition and this guide will spark an interest in contemporary history. More than that, we wish to enter into a dialogue with our visitors. In contrast to many other museums, we have attempted to integrate a hands-on approach to our subject, suitable for both those with and without prior knowledge of the East German system. This approach has established our reputation as one of the most interactive museums in Europe – both sections of our exhibition were nominated for the highly-prestigious European Museum of the Year Award in both 2008 and 2012.

Not just a guide to our exhibition, this book also hopes to introduce our readers to the GDR itself. Its contents represent the fruit of a process of exchange between the historians Dr. Stefan Wolle and Dr. Jochen Voit, the journalist Andreas Menn, our curator Katrin Strohl and myself. This profitable collaboration has produced texts of both impeccable reliability and, we hope, the ability to fascinate and amuse.

Come with us on an exciting journey of discovery through the GDR. I wish you an interesting and fun experience in the exhibition and with our guidebook!

Sincerely, Robert Rückel
Berlin, April 2012

TABLE OF CONTENTS

»A HANDS-ON EXPERIENCE OF EVERYDAY LIFE IN A BYGONE STATE«

The townscape of the GDR was dominated by high-rise tower blocks – first loved, then hated, these »cupboards for people« provided a home for millions of East Germans, who lived, loved and dreamt within their confines. Large-scale building schemes resulted in the emergence of extensive housing estates, such as Halle New Town and Berlin Hellersdorf, on the edges of towns and cities. The first section of our exhibition reproduces a tower block housing estate on a scale of 1:20.

The cabinets represent tower blocks of the »Series 70«, the most common building system used in the GDR. A walk-in dolls' house seems at first to be a somewhat odd approach, but gives an authentic impression of the grey world of its role model. While it provides a dreary first impression, it is actually the cover for a more lively culture of every-day life. The flats serve both as space dividers and exhibition cabinets. It is only after the visitors begin to use the installations that they give an insight into the private life of a GDR citizen. Once in this world, films, new media, drawers and cabinets filled with exhibition pieces and diorama tell the story of life in a defunct state.

The stone-grey facades of the high-rise flats are mass-produced, just like their role models. Moving from flat to flat, the visitor moves from topic 1 to 16, examining the death strip on the Berlin Wall, a typical GDR child's bedroom, reading a diary of shortages, rummaging through a wardrobe full of plastic clothes, or watching children's television.

These are not the only interactive objects: the reproduction of a flat with a living room, kitchen and bathroom in 1970s design invites you to look through drawers, switch the television to the (forbidden) West German channels or to talk to your despairing neighbour on the telephone. All too much for you? Why not relax in a simulation of a leisurely Trabi ride or enjoy a GDR newsreel on authentic cinema seats.

With red ceilings and pillars and collectivist slogans daubed on the wall, the influence of Socialism is pervasive. Located in the former Palast Hotel, one of the best hotels in the GDR, something of the former ideological atmosphere remains.

»BEHIND THE FAÇADE OF POWER«

Penetrating the »fog-screen of the bureaucracy,« the visitor enters the semi-circle of power. At the head of the room and under the gaze of the patron saints of Socialism, Marx, Engels and Lenin, is the conference table of the mighty SED. Taking their place at the table, the visitor can operate the touch-screen to access information regarding the life and working of the party.

In the first semi-circle around this »centre of power«, the exhibition outlines the instruments of Party rule including the Federation of Unions, the National Front and the youth organizations. Lenin's dictum that the »unions are the transmission belt of the Party« is demonstrated in a hands-on fashion and the pseudo-pluralism of the GDR parliament is also unmasked in a surprising way. Thus informed, the visitor can now try and find a way to cast a truly free and fair vote in the general election. The second semi-circle is dominated by large-format propaganda photographs. The GDR citizens (and hence the visitor) are shown what the SED wants them to see: the triumphant mining industry, the celebratory inauguration of the new »democratic« constitution, the »defensive« People's Army and the inseparable bond of love with their Socialist brother states.

Just as the average East German citizen was able to read between the lines of the official party newspapers, the visitor is also able to delve behind the official façade. Behind the propaganda photos are doors and draws with exhibits, explanations and multi-media installations which reveal the reality of life in the GDR. Visitors can read stories about visits from the West, become the manager of a Trabant factory, read about the birth of the GDR and experience life in the National People's Army. They can even try out their Russian skills. The rear-side of the room divider affords even deeper insights into the functioning of the SED dictatorship, addressing the very topics that the SED sought to hide from their citizens: automatic guns and mines on the border, environmental destruction, difficult relations with the Eastern bloc and the perfidious militarization of kindergartens and schools.

Hidden at the far end of the room are a variety of installations dealing with a number of top-secret matters about which the ordinary citizen was oblivious. The privileges of the Party elite and the opposition movement and its repression now become visible. Drawn into this secret world, the visitor can sit in a ministerial Volvo and start a virtual tour through East Berlin, or study the growth of the opposition movement. A reconstructed interrogation room transforms the visitor into a suspect, and from an uncomfortable position, you can listen to the reconstructed interrogation through your elbows and hands.

Following the peaceful revolution, you can leave the GDR through a hole in the wall.

FOCUSING ON THE PERSON

Chief historian Dr. Stefan Wolle

Almost every household has a suitcase or box filled with memories. Sometimes its owner even rummages through the souvenirs of their life, each object recalling fragments of the past. Travellers on such journeys of discovery unearth items of considerable oddity – train timetables for decommissioned lines, worthless coins and electrical devices with obsolete plugs. All objects of no practical value but which all recount a very personal story. Even the symbols of the long-defunct SED regime can provide a strangely comforting feeling. Such items are many and various: a pennant or paper flag; a pioneer neck scarf; a FDJ shirt; a »Book of Good Deeds« recording the owner's achievements in the collection of waste paper; or a Brigade scrapbook recording an excursion. Such items resemble the shards of a broken mirror which once broken are difficult to piece together.

The historical consensus is both clear and in little need of revision. The GDR was a Soviet satellite held together by the grip of its security apparatus. The planned economy proved itself inferior to the free market and the generous social system was not only unsustainable but contributed to the collapse of the system as a whole. The regime was removed by a democratic mass movement in 1989 and the reunification with West Germany was endorsed by a large majority of East Germans.

Many seek to use this consensus to »close the file« on the GDR. Yet to do so would leave many questions unanswered. The GDR was more than an artifice of ideology and power; it involved the lives of millions of people. Growing up in the GDR, they went to school, served in the »armed organs«, and worked, lived and raised families. Life in the GDR could be very happy away from the often distant politics and ideology.

Nevertheless, living with the conditions of scarcity and the considerable competition for goods was far from ideal. All were forced to develop some response to the conditions and barter, moonlighting and the black market thrived. Many retreated into their private worlds, making the holiday home the symbol of life in the GDR. The division between a personal and a public opinion was almost unavoidable; the fear of drawing attention to oneself, or worse, coming into conflict with the Stasi were important parts of everyday life.

None of this could have been mastered without the considerable resources of humour, optimism and cheerfulness which were to be found under Real Existing Socialism. This explains why so many are prepared to joke about their lives in the GDR, even if the laughter sometimes gets stuck in their throats. One of the more popular SED slogans was their claim to »focus on the person«. This was never anything but a hollow phrase; the SED focussed on nothing other than retaining power. However, in looking back at the history of the GDR let us take up this slogan. After all, the state was made up of the people living in it.

A STATE COMES ...

In the beginning was defeat. With the signature of unconditional surrender by the German Empire on 8 May 1945, the close of the Second World War brought the total destruction of its originator. Dividing Germany into four zones of occupation, the victorious allies – the USA, Great Britain, France and the Soviet Union – all set the tone in their own sphere of influence. Despite the initial popularity of a number of Soviet measures (such as a wide-reaching land reform) the Soviet Zone of Occupation soon developed into a Communist dictatorship under the leadership of the Socialist Unity Party of Germany (SED).

Founded in 7 October 1949, the German Democratic Republic (GDR) never enjoyed any level of popular consent. Popular disaffection over poor living

Above *The foundation of the GDR on 7/10/1949; SED emblem; The people's uprising on 17 June 1953; Walter Ulbricht, Chairman of the State Council 1960 – 1973*

conditions and repression culminated in mass strikes and demonstrations on 17 June 1953; only Soviet tanks prevented a revolution. Unhappy at the prevailing conditions, ever-more East Germans (especially the well-educated) voted with their feet and fled to West Germany. Alarmed at the prospect of losing his most valuable workers, Walther Ulbricht obtained Soviet permission to seal off the last remaining gap in the iron curtain. The building of the Berlin Wall (13 August 1961) left East Germans trapped in the GDR.

Forced to make the best of a changed situation, people set about building themselves a life. The SED leadership sought to help them in their endeavour and set about modernizing society, promising greater prosperity,

Below The Berlin Wall at the Reichstag; Erich Honecker, Chairman of the State Council 1976 – 1989; Leonid Brezhnev and Erich Honecker; 30th anniversary of the GDR, 1979

artistic freedoms and less repression. Nevertheless, wide-spread hopes of achieving »Socialism with a human face« were decisively and finally dashed on 21 August 1968, following the military repression of the Prague Spring in Czechoslovakia.

Having achieved widespread international recognition in the 1970s, the SED felt forced to initiate reforms aimed at engineering an apparently more open society, whilst expanding the security apparatus. A comprehensive programme of social provision launched in a bid to stabilize the system led only to massive debt and the threat of bankruptcy.

This situation was compounded by the popular hopes raised in the GDR by Michael Gorbachev's programme of

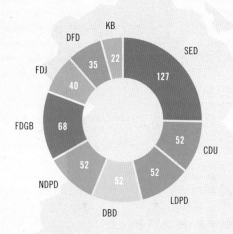

THE GDR PARLIAMENT
COMPOSITION IN THE EIGHTH LEGISLATIVE PERIOD 1981–1986

KB 22
DFD 35
FDJ 40
FDGB 68
SED 127
CDU 52
LDPD 52
DBD 52
NDPD 52

■	SED	Socialist Unity Party of Germany
■	CDU	Christian Democratic Union of Germany
■	LDPD	Liberal Democratic Party of Germany
■	DBD	Democratic Peasants' Party of Germany
■	NDPD	National Democratic Party of Germany
■	FDGB	Free German Trade Union Federation
■	FDJ	Free German Youth
■	DFD	The Democratic Women's League of Germany
■	KB	League of Culture

... AND GOES

reform. The latent crisis of GDR Socialism now became acute, threatening its very existence. With a group of dissidents crystallizing under the protection of the Lutheran Church, the cry for human rights and freedom became loud. The celebrations to mark the fortieth anniversary of the GDR held in October 1989 were overshadowed by mass demonstrations in Leipzig, Berlin and other large cities. The marchers called for democracy, freedom and reform.

The sheer number of protestors forced the overwhelmed border guards to open the border to West Berlin.

A peaceful revolution had swept away SED Socialism, bringing freedom and democracy. With the reunification of the two Germanys, the GDR had finally been consigned to history.

Above Peace prayers in Gera, 26.10.1989; a Monday demonstration in Leipzig, 16.10.1989
Below A demonstration in Erfurt, 26.10.1989; The West German embassy in Prague, Sep. 1989

DIVIDE AND RULE

The border dividing the two Germanys was seen not just on maps but carved into the landscape. It was an impermeable fortress running from North to South through a once unified land. In the 1950s, East Germans wishing to move Westwards could travel to divided Berlin and cross to the Western sector. Split into four sectors and administered jointly by the victorious allies – Great Britain, the USA, France and the Soviet Union – Berlin assumed an island status during the Cold War. With the East-West border open until 1961, it was relatively easy to pass between the sectors. As a result, over 2.6 million GDR citizens fled to the West via West Berlin. Faced with this damaging haemorrhage of valuable workers, the SED leadership decided to seal the border on 13 August 1961.

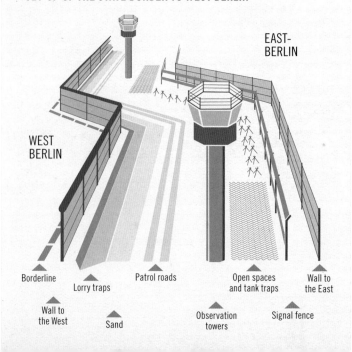

SET-UP OF THE STATE BORDER TO WEST BERLIN

EAST-BERLIN

WEST BERLIN

Borderline

Lorry traps

Patrol roads

Open spaces and tank traps

Wall to the East

Wall to the West

Sand

Observation towers

Signal fence

Completing and perfecting the separation between East and West, the Berlin Wall was subject to systematic extension. Starting as a simple wall, it soon developed into a graduated system of frontier control designed to prevent any and all attempts at escape. The order to shoot was issued from the beginning. The consequence was 136 proven deaths between 1961 and 1989.

The closure of the border had initially prevented West Berliners from visiting their Eastern friends and relatives, a situation which changed only after the beginnings of détente. 1963 saw the first Christmas in which West Berliners could visit their relatives in the East. The Basic Treaty of 1971 introduced a visa system under which West Berliners were permitted to visit East Berlin for a day, returning before midnight. The treaty also stabilized the legal position of the roads between West Berlin and West Germany. Despite all these changes, ordinary East Germans remained trapped behind »their« wall. The absurdity of the division of Berlin gradually became normality.

Left *Diorama of the border area in the exhibition* **Right** *The course of the border in Berlin*

CARDBOARD COMRADE

The mechanisms of the ticket machines for regional trains had a highly idiosyncratic construction: the coin slot and ticket dispenser were actually constructed separately from each other. The result was that you could pay the 20 Pfennig fare but it was not entirely necessary. Other methods of transport in the GDR were not free but were still inexpensive. This did not make them reliable. The trains of the »Imperial German Railways«, (itself an anachronism in a Socialist society) were dirty and full. A single flake of snow was often sufficient to result in disruptions and cancelled trains due to »extreme weather conditions«. Passengers on the bus and tram networks could tell a similar story. Forty years of minimal investment in the transport system produced a uniform popular wish: everybody wanted a car.

The ›Trabi‹ was not the only car on offer: the Wartburg was manufactured in Eisenach, and Socialist brother states delivered Škodas and Ladas. Nevertheless, the leading figures of the republic preferred the Western luxury model Volvo. Despite such variety, the ›Trabi‹ remained the uncontested symbol of East German mobility.

A Russian word meaning »companion«, many ›Trabis‹ remained a trusted friend to many East Germans, first as a

PRIVATE CARS ACCORDING TO TYPE, 1988

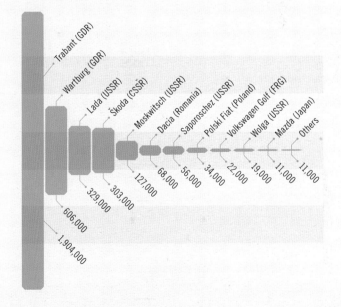

Trabant (GDR) 1,904,000
Wartburg (GDR) 606,000
Lada (USSR) 329,000
Škoda (CSSR) 303,000
Moskwitsch (USSR) 127,000
Dacia (Romania) 68,000
Saporoschez (USSR) 56,000
Polski Fiat (Poland) 34,000
Volkswagen Golf (FRG) 22,000
Wolga (USSR) 19,000
Mazda (Japan) 11,000
Others 11,000

dream (waiting times for the car could stretch to 16 years) and then as a status symbol and a hobby. The construction of this »cardboard box with an engine« was so simple that the happy owner was usually able to repair the majority of faults themselves. Made of Duroplast, a mixture of cotton felt and plastic, the housing was lightweight, rust-free and saved expensive metal imports. Should the traveller have ambitious plans – such as a trip to Bulgaria – he would be careful to take the requisite tools and mechanical manuals so as to ensure a safe return. Partly because they required so much attention, the driver often developed a strong and trusting bond with his car.

The more committed driver could even buy records about his car such as the famous refrain »A sky blue Trabant, driving through the countryside ...« or tell jokes. One of the best: »what do you call a ›Trabi‹ on a hill? – A miracle!«

■ A CAR PURCHASE CONTRACT, 1968

Trabant P 601 in the exhibition

WESTERN LINES UNDER EAST BERLIN

The Berlin Wall divided not just a city but also a number of its traffic routes. East German maps soon expunged all train, bus and tram routes going West and the whole of West Berlin was replaced with a light grey blank. Despite their official non-existence, many trains from West Berlin continued to travel under the GDR capital — one example being the South-North S-Bahn line which had to cross very centre of East Berlin. Passengers of the S2 (today's S1) and the underground lines U6 and U8 were informed by loudspeaker »Last station in West Berlin! Last station in West Berlin!«. The trains then rumbled through (or better under) Socialism, inching past abandoned stations apparently trapped in a 1960s time-warp. They were well guarded: halting or alighting was strictly forbidden.

S-Bahn stations Potsdamer Platz, 1990

GHOST STATIONS
ABANDONNED STATIONS UNDER EAST BERLIN

● S-Bahn West Berlin   ● S-Bahn East Berlin

■ Underground railway West Berlin   ▨ Underground railway East Berlin

▢ Ghost station – station in East Berlin where the trains did not stop

U8   S2   A

Schönhauser Allee

Gesundbrunnen

U6

Reinickendorfer-Str.

Bernauer Str.

WEST
BERLIN

EAST
BERLIN

Oranienburger Str.

Lehrter Stadtbanhof

Stadtbahn

Friedrichstr.   Alexanderplatz

Unter den Linden   Jannowitzbrücke

Potsdamer Platz   Heinrich-Heine-Str.

Kochstr.

Moritzplatz

S2   U6   U8

Below U-Bahn Station Bernauer Strasse
Workers open the entrance with
pneumatic drills, 1990

Poster »NATO Agents Don't Stand a Chance«
Poster for a Stasi exhibition in the Berolina-Haus
on the Alexanderplatz in 1961. Found in the closed
underground station Stadtmitte, 1990.

Above Friedrichstraße station in 1990: divided
Centre Friedrichstraße as a terminus

There were only two exceptions: despite its location in Eastern territory, the entrance of the S-Bahn station Wollankstraße opened to West Berlin. Friedrichstraße station on the other hand was separated into a Western and an Eastern half despite being located entirely in East Berlin. The Eastern platforms served normal East German commuter traffic; passengers arriving at the Western platform had two choices: either to take the next train to West Berlin or to enter East Berlin via the border crossing in the so-called Palace of Tears. All other exits were bricked up.

»BE HAPPY AND SING«

Being young in the GDR could be fun if you had the nerve and resourcefulness: illegal camping on the Baltic Sea, swimming at night (strictly forbidden) hanging around at the petrol station; making your own clothes, taping Radio ›DR 64‹ and racing dangerously on your Simson motor scooter. Yet it also meant Pioneer afternoons, collecting scrap and working in the Free German Youth (FDJ) harvest brigade. Such activities were not obligatory, but could be helpful if you wanted to go to university. Besides, the FDJ camp was the best place to find your first sweetheart. Growing up was regulated by a clear timetable with a lot of oath swearing. Entry to the Pioneers aged 6, promotion to the Thälmann Pioneers aged 9 and declared an adult at the youth dedication ceremony aged 14. The state listened carefully to the vows made at such ceremonies, whereas the participants were more interested in the presents that they would receive. Further education towards becoming a rounded Socialist citizen was

Till Böttcher working the printing press in the Umweltbibliothek, 1989

provided by the FDJ, which organized seminars, group meetings and festivals. More exclusive was membership of the Society for Sport and Technology (GST) which combined pre-military training with extreme sports – but only for boys.

Youth in the GDR was also inseparably associated with the eternal hunt for jeans, trainers and records from the West and with the Beat Movement and the East German bands the Puhdys and Karat. Real rebellion such as that pursued in the ›Umweltbibliothek‹ was restricted to a few exceptional people; the Socialist upbringing was successful in the majority of cases. For many, their youth was over extremely quickly as a number of state incentives moved people to settle down and start a family at a relatively young age. All that was left of this glorious but short period of youth was a number of (copied) cassettes, a blue FDJ shirt (too small) and school books with a name clearly printed on the front.

»LEARN, LEARN AND LEARN AGAIN« W. I. LENIN

Monday morning in many school yards heard the same cry: »Comrade Principal, the school is assembled!«. The flag rising slowly, hundreds of school children sang a pioneer song. Education was conceived as the formation of a Socialist citizen and teaching in the social sciences (and other subjects) was dominated by the regurgitation of prescribed wisdom. Even the theses of the classic authors of Marxist Leninism were reduced to a set of stock phrases. University courses repeated exactly the same propositions within the scope of a compulsory basic course tested in both written and oral examinations. Those taking a doctoral degree were forced to repeat the material for a third time.

Achievement was very important, and standards were high, especially in Mathematics and the Natural Sciences. Moreover, school did not finish with the last lesson; some investigated their surroundings in the guise of »young scientists«, whilst others swotted for the Mathematics Olympia. The more sporting opted to train in the gym for a zero gravity life as a cosmonaut. Indeed, sport and military training was accorded a prominent place in young people's lives. Sport lessons functioned as pre-military training in another guise and the Society for Sport and Technology (GST) instructed its charges in shooting and marching. Even university students were subject to weekly (obligatory) sport courses with an examination culminating in a dive from the five-metre board. Every male student was forced to complete a month-long military camp; females had to complete a course in civil defence.

The GDR education system produced successful athletes, good soldiers, industrious engineers and well-qualified scientists. Yet for all its academic-mindedness, the system frowned on critical thinking. In 1988, the expulsion of four Berlin school children caused uproar. In a critical article on the official school wall newspaper, they questioned the sense of the annual military parades. Attracting widespread publicity from civil rights activists and the Western media, this case was only one of many such disciplinary actions which had previously gone unnoticed.

THE FURTHER CAREERS OF 16 YEAR OLDS IN 1989

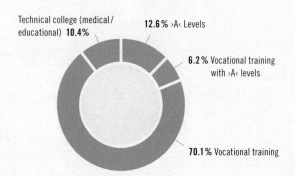

Technical college (medical/educational) **10.4%**

12.6% ›A‹ Levels

6.2% Vocational training with ›A‹ levels

70.1% Vocational training

LEVELS OF POPULAR QUALIFICATION (FROM 14) 1989

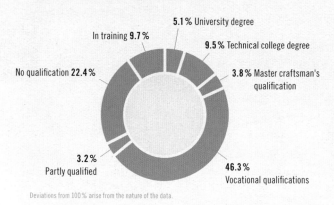

In training **9.7%**

5.1% University degree

9.5% Technical college degree

3.8% Master craftsman's qualification

No qualification **22.4%**

3.2% Partly qualified

46.3% Vocational qualifications

Deviations from 100% arise from the nature of the data.

■ **THE SCHOOL SYSTEM IN THE GDR**
- ■ POLYTECHNIC SCHOOL (POS): obligatory until the age of 14
- ■ EXTENDED SECONDARY SCHOOL (EOS): for the ages 16–18 resulting in ›A‹ levels
- ■ SCHOOLS OF VOCATIONAL TRAINING: three-year college and practice-based training following the POS
- ■ VOCATIONAL SCHOOLS (MEDICAL-EDUCATIONAL): three-year courses following the POS for careers such as medical assistant or nursery teacher
- ■ TECHNICHAL COLLEGE (TECHNICAL-ECONOMIC): three-year courses providing vocational training for engineering jobs (without degree)
- ■ UNIVERSITY: five-year course of study

STARTING EARLY

Childcare provision in the GDR was exemplary. Seeking to exploit the employment potential of women, the state provided a sufficient number of crèche and Kindergarten places to enable mothers to work. This also enabled the state to begin early with the work of raising its children to become model Socialist citizens. Learning to count using toy tanks and soldiers was no rare occurrence. Seeking to bring children out of their nappies as early as possible, nursery teachers left their charges together on the long potty bench until they were all finished — no-one could get up until the last had »gone.« Writing in the 1990s, the West German criminologist Christian Pfeiffer identified such practices as a possible source of Right-Wing extremism in East Germany. This so-called »potty debate« soon blew over, and potty banks are still to be found in a number crèches across Eastern Germany.

NUMBER OF CRÈCHE PLACES
PER 1,000 CHILDREN

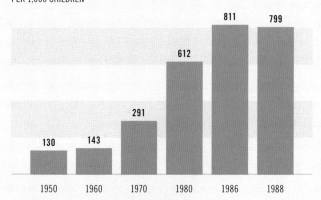

1950	1960	1970	1980	1986	1988
130	143	291	612	811	799

THE DREAM OF FULL EMPLOYMENT

SALES ASSISTANT

Training: school until 14, two and a half years vocational training

Monthly earnings 1988:
600 – 800 Marks

BRICKLAYER

Training: school until 16, two years vocational training

Monthly earnings 1988:
1,110 – 1,370 Marks

FARMER »Technician for livestock production«

Training: school until 16, two years vocational training resulting in ›A‹ levels

Monthly earnings 1988:
1,197 Marks

Marks

FARMER »Technician for arable production«

Training: school until 16, two years vocational training resulting in ›A‹ levels

Monthly earnings 1988:
1,197 Marks

Life in the GDR focussed on work. Every citizen had a job, and those refusing to work were punished for their anti-social behaviour. School children learnt about the world of work in their weekly »day of lessons in production« – an invitation to various work situations to learn about the theory and practice of the planned economy. The employer or ›company‹ was much more than a source of money, it was also a universal provider. It provided accommodation, hospitals, a crèche, and even holidays. Indeed, such company facilities were often better equipped than their municipal counterparts. Many people came to see their job as a second home and it was not unusual that a worker would remain with an employer for his whole life. Colleagues in the ›work brigade‹ were more often than not one's friends after work, and went out and travelled together. If a worker absented himself from work, his ›mates‹ would often try and find out why.

CHEMICHAL ENGINEER

Training: school until 18 and
a university degree (5 years)

Monthly earnings 1988:
1,000 – 1,300 Marks

ENGINEER

Training: school until 16, two years vocational
training, Vocational school (2 – 3 years) or
school until 18 and a university degree (5 years)

Monthly earnings 1988: 1,470 Marks

MINER

Training: school until 14,
three-year vocational training

Monthly earnings 1988:
1,167 – 1,444 Marks

Life in the countryside changed radically. After the forced collectivization of small farms into huge »Agricultural Production Collectives«, the former farmers were called Technicians for Livestock or Arable Production and assigned to small areas of specialization. Farms had become factories.

The largest companies operated »halls of fame« – large pin boards on which the picture of the best performing employees were displayed. The faces thus displayed belonged to those workers had met or even exceeded their targets. Quick work was also rewarded with a bonus, medal or even a title. The rewards were much-coveted and vying for their bestowal replaced the competition of the free market. The titles and medals have long been consigned to the archive – free market competition is back and so is unemployment.

SOLD OUT

There was a joke: »everything is available but not always, and not everywhere and certainly not when you need it.« The most advanced of the Eastern Bloc nations, the GDR economy produced goods of international quality. Nevertheless, this fact did not manifest itself in the shops and shopping centres of East Germany.

One week letter writers could not buy paper or envelopes, the next saw an acute shortage of honey or crisp bread. Fruit and vegetables were always scarce – not just exotic fruits but even tomatoes and cucumbers. Meat and cured meat needed for the weekend was best bought on a Thursday. The shortages were the result of the planned economy, inefficient production and a cumbersome bureaucracy. The central allocation of all goods meant that they often did not arrive where they were needed. Some products were rarely seen because they disappeared abroad as exports.

If West German consumers went on the hunt for bargains, GDR shoppers were always on the lookout for scarce goods. Always »with their eyes peeled«, people would never leave the house without a shopping bag »just in case«.

The customer no longer bought what they needed, but what was there. Scarcity did not encourage economy; rather it engendered waste. Prices were fixed not according to supply and demand, but were set by the state and often even heavily subsidized. Rent, electricity, gas, water and a number of basic foodstuffs were so cheap that people were often over-generous in their use.

During the last years of Socialism, there were few products which were readily available and shop assistants introduced a system of rationing. Cotton nappies or children's underwear were only released upon presentation of an identity card. Many mothers presented their children as proof of need.

›HANDELSORGANISATION‹ (RETAIL ORGANISATIONS)

›CENTRUM‹ DEPARTMENT STORES

- Located in many large and medium-sized towns and cities
- Providing a wide range of products
- The largest was located on Berlin's Alexanderplatz

THE ›CENTRUM‹ MAIL ORDER HOUSE

- A large mail-order company located in Leipzig
- In 1972, it despatched 50,000 packages per day

›EXQUISIT‹ AND ›DELIKAT‹ STORES

- Located in a number of East German towns since 1978
- Sold expensive clothes and foodstuffs of good quality
- Often imported from the »Non-Socialist Economic Area« (NSW)

›INTERSHOPS‹

- Located at border crossings and airports
- Sold duty-free products purchasable with foreign currency
- From 1979, GDR citizens had to pay with »forum cheques«

›KONSUMGENOSSENSCHAF‹ (KONSUMENT CO-OPERATIVES)

›KONSUMENT‹ DEPARTMENT STORES

- In almost every town or city
- Customers collected coupons to receive an end of year payment

›KONSUMENT‹ MAIL ORDER COMPANY

- Located in Karl-Marx-Stadt (Chemnitz)
- Provided a very wide range of products
- Closed in 1976 due to shortages

THE ›GENEX‹ MAIL ORDER COMPANY

PRESENTS AND SMALL EXPORTS LTD.

- Established in 1956 to gather foreign currency
- Foreigners could order products to be delivered to GDR citizens

NATIONALLY OWNED PRODUCTS

The name of the products on the supermarket shelves promised a world of glamour hardly distinguishable from the Western advertisements. Bicycles were named ›Diamant‹ (Diamond), wall units ›Karat‹ and a popular brandy went under the name ›Goldkrone‹. Smokers puffed on ›Juwel‹ (Jewel) cigarettes and all manner of broken implements were fixed with ›Rapid‹ instant glue. The GDR economy also offered a whole host of instant products including ›Tempo-Linsen‹ (Tempo Lentils), coffee power ›Im Nu‹ (literally meaning »in a fix«) or even ›Kurzkoch Reis‹ (Quick Rice).

All this modernity and rationality suggested by the names was designed to make a housewife's life considerably easier. Despite such inferred promises, consumers watched the adverts on West German television with wide eyes.

The highest praise for Eastern products – if meant only ironically – was the epithet ›just like a Western product‹.

Packets sent from West Germany ensured steady stream of Western consumer products into the GDR. Initially angered by this Western cultural influence, the SED sought to stigmatize it: Western fashion was frowned upon and school teachers reprimanded any of their charges found writing with West German pens or stationary. Posters of West German pop stars or footballers were even confiscated.

The later years of the GDR saw a relaxation of attitudes, as it was recognized that this small-scale practice of private imports served to relieve the hard-pressed GDR retail sector. The GDR authorities were happiest if Western money was used to buy goods from the ›Intershops‹. Foreign currency spent in this equivalent to a duty free shop allowed the purchase of tax-free Western goods and a little bit of international flair.

HONECKER VISITS THE PORCELLAN FACTORY IN MEISSEN. A SHEEPISH DIRECTOR TELLS HIM:

»FIVE PERCENT OF OUR PRODUCTION CONSISTS OF REJECTS.«

HONECKER IS WORRIED:

»IS THAT ENOUGH TO SUPPLY OUR POPULATION?«

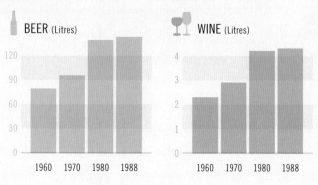

THE PER CAPITA CONSUMPTION OF SELECTED STIMULANTS

BEER (Litres)

	1960	1970	1980	1988

WINE (Litres)

	1960	1970	1980	1988

KRUSTA WITH BULL'S BLOOD

Alcohol was the drug of choice in the GDR. With an estimated per capita consumption of 16 litres of pure alcohol per year, the men and women of the GDR could drink all-comers under the table. 16 litres equates to some 286 bottles of beer and 23 bottles of spirits per person. Abandoning the traditional German law regulating alcohol quality (the famous ›Reinheitsgebot‹), the wide variety of ingredients used (semolina, lactic acid or silica gel compounds) gave every brand its own characteristic taste. Quality wines from Saxony were reserved for state banquets, whilst the working class drank Bull's Blood, Donkey's Milk and Balkan Fire imported from Yugoslavia, Bulgaria and Hungary. Those in search of truly hard drink turned to a host of products with such promising names as ›Goldi‹, ›Primasprit‹, ›Gotano‹ or the ›Blue Strangler‹. The only places where alcohol consumption was forbidden were on the road and in the army. Motorists could sweeten their journey with the alcohol-free beer ›Aubi‹. It might have improved their driving skills, but did not taste good.

Restaurant patrons needed a great deal of patience. Queuing in front of the sign informing them to »wait here to be assigned a table!« guests (for one of the many free tables)

SPIRITS (Litres)

	1960	1970	1980	1988

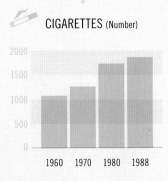

CIGARETTES (Number)

	1960	1970	1980	1988

could be subject to a long wait. Feeling powerful, waiters were often given to turning guests away even though the tables were free. Roast chicken, referred to as ›Goldbroiler‹ was a popular takeaway meal sold on the street. Derived from the English verb »to broil«, the meal was a rarity in the GDR diet – a dish with an English name in a country which eschewed all things Anglo-Saxon. It was such preferences which led to the Germanization of a range of American dishes – the Hamburger was transformed into a ›Grilletta‹, the Hot Dog was sold as a ›Ketwurst‹ (a combination of ketchup and the German word for Sausage). Unable or unwilling to provide that symbol of capitalist consumption, Coca-Cola was replaced with ›Club-Cola‹ or ›Vita-Cola‹ served with a dash of lemon and a lot of fizzy water. The East German food industry was very resourceful: during times of meat shortage, the cook took a slice of sausage meat and fried it with spaghetti and tomato sauce: the Hunter's Steak! Leftovers were turned into Soljanka, a Russian soup made of meat, bacon, onions and gherkin.

FROM THE RUINS RISEN NEWLY

Berlin-Hellersdorf

PERCENTAGE OF GDR FLATS
WITH THE FOLLOWING AMENITIES

		1971	1989
	Bath / shower	39	82
	Inside toilet	36	76
	Modern heating	11	47
	Telephone	8	16

A visitor to the GDR would be surprised to find bombed-out houses, shrapnel embedded in house facades and signs pointing the way to the air raid shelter, even long after the war. Some of this damage even remained when the GDR fell in 1989. Despite such evidence of urban neglect, the authorities commissioned an endless stream of songs and slogans emphasising their achievements in reconstruction. Marching in the 1950s and 60s, the Free German Youth missed no opportunity to sing their popular song »Rebuild!, Rebuild! Let the Free German Youth Rebuild!«

Nevertheless, the building activities of the 1950s and 60s of which they sang so enthusiastically were purely for show. A number of high-prestige building projects in Berlin, Leipzig, Dresden and the other district capitals involving such monumental edifices as the Television Tower and the hotel on the Alexanderplatz all proclaimed the success of Socialism but did little to relieve the chronic housing shortage. This was addressed only at the beginning of the 1970s.

A large-scale housing programme saw a number of high-rise tower block housing estates suddenly appear on the edge of large towns and cities. The new flats were in high demand and those who actually moved in to such dwellings could count themselves lucky. The renovation of older houses was also stepped up, but the paucity of resources meant that only prestige objects were improved in this way.

The flagship project of renovation was the Nikolaiviertel in Berlin, a mixture of period-style tower blocks and a very few renovated historic buildings. Away from the international gaze, the ordinary older towns were left to decay. In an allusion to the official peace propaganda, some humorists spoke of »creating ruins without weapons«. The housing shortage was a never-ending problem, as the ridiculously low rents enabled married couples to retain large flats and houses even after their children had flown the nest — a market economy would have forced them to look for cheaper accommodation.

CUPBOARDS FOR PEOPLE

WBS 70 is the abbreviation for ›Wohnungsbauserie 70‹, the most commonly erected series of tower blocks used in in the GDR. Working under the aegis of the large-scale housing programme launched in 1971, the state erected over 1.5 million tower blocks built from prefabricated concrete panels, 42 % of which were of the series WBS 70. As a result, this became a synonym for all new blocks of flats. Every flat had its own (indoor) bathroom referred to as a plumbing unit and was connected to a district heating network. Compared to the old houses with their toilet in the stairwell and coal-fired radiators, the new flats provided unheard-of luxury at a low price; the average household spent 2.4 % of its income on rent.

HOME SWEET HOME

With the shift in emphasis from building eye-catching city centres to out-of-town high-rise settlements at the beginning of the 1970s, all those wanting a new flat had to make their way to the housing office. The state monopoly of housing allocation meant that flat-hunters needed patience, good connections and no small portion of luck. After a few years, those thus-endowed were allocated one of the much-coveted

A living room in Dessau, 1981

»full-comfort« flats. The facilities in the existing blocks of flats remained on a level with the pre-war years: a coal-fired radiator, no bathroom, a WC in the stairwell, simple windows and damp walls. Nothing changed much in this segment of the market, as concentrating on high-prestige buildings, the construction programme of the 1950s and 60s brought very few new flats. As a result, the lack of housing became the central problem which the SED was forced to address.

The process of moving in to a new flat was always celebrated in style. The move meant an end to the need to hump coal or fire-wood up many flights of stairs or to rush off in the middle of the night to the communal toilet. No longer were babies bathed in the kitchen. Moreover, the price of such progress was not high; as with all the other basic

costs of living, the rents were heavily subsidized.

The inhabitants of this new domestic paradise set about furnishing their homes with great care and gusto. Especially popular were a common three-piece suite with an equally common adjustable »multifunction table«. No flat was complete without the obligatory sofa bed for the regular visitors which such households always attracted. This was rounded off by thick, soft carpets, heavy drapes and net curtains. The ›Karat‹ wall unit was also a must for every housewife, the majority of whom could only afford such luxury on hire purchase.

The identical form of the majority of flats in the GDR meant that furniture was produced according to unitary dimensions. Although practical, it meant that everybody's house looked similar.

Reconstruction of a living room in Berlin, 2006

Not blind to this obvious fact, people invested much time and care to affect a certain level of individuality. The scene of the greatest individualism was the balcony – turned into a half-timbered structure and decorated with carriage wheels, horse shoes, spirit lamps and other such homespun objects. The average occupant needed good DIY skills as workmen were in short supply. Carpentry, painting, plumbing, tiling and wall-paper hanging were all taught at school. To enjoy their living room, the average GDR citizen first had to construct it.

Für Arbeiten, die im Knien zu verrichten si
45 cm), das man selbst anfertigen und mit e
kann.

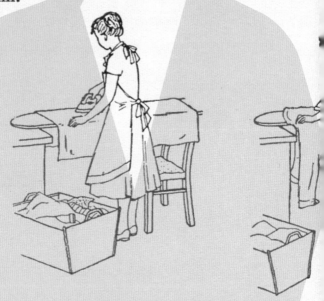

Gleichmäßige anstrengende Arbeit lä

Lasten soll man vom Boden mit gebeugten
leichter als mit einem, am leichtesten dann, w

BE

Bettgestell. Bei einer gründlichen Säuberun
zunehmen ist, werden Deckbetten, Decken un
Das Gestell wird von allen Seiten sorgfältig ger
den Möbel (s. S. 358) verfährt.

Matratzen. Den Rahmen der *Sprungfederm*
man mit dem Pinsel ab. *Kastenmatratzen* kann
bürsten. Auch die *Auflegematratzen* werden am
ist zu vermeiden, da es der Füllung schadet.
wenn sie öfter gegeneinander ausgewechselt we
nicht erst Vertiefungen einliegen. Es empfiehl
Decke auf die *Sprungfedermatratze zu legen. F*
Matratzenschoner an.

npfiehlt sich ein kleines Polster (etwa 30 mal
abwaschbaren Überzug aus Plastfolie versehen

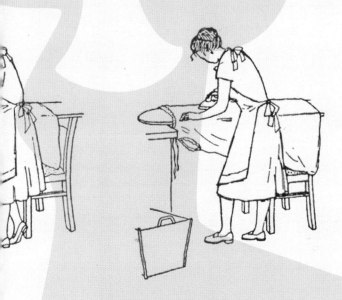

Leistungsfähigkeit schnell absinken

hochheben. Das Tragen mit zwei Armen ist
ie Lasten nahe am Körper gehalten werden.

N

Betten, die mindestens einmal im Jahr vor-
tratzen aus dem Bettgestell herausgenommen.
, wobei man wie bei der Pflege der entsprechen-

n wischt man feucht ab, die Spiralen staubt
von beiden Seiten absaugen oder kräftig ab-
n von allen Seiten abgesaugt; heftiges Klopfen
einzelnen Teile der Aufleger werden geschont,
damit sich an den stark beanspruchten Stellen
, zum Schutz der Auflegematratzen *eine dicke*
schäfte *fertigen für diesen Zweck auch* spezielle

EQUALITY – SOMETIMES

According to article 38 of the GDR constitution, the »family is the smallest cell of society.« Humorists at weddings were wont to add to this sentence »and it is in this smallest of cells that you will be sitting for the rest of your life!« Not just a joke in poor taste, it was also statistically incorrect, as divorce rates in the GDR were relatively high. An East German marriage was considerably less binding than a West German marriage; not only did East Germans marry much earlier than their Western cousins, but divorces were much easier to obtain. One result was a high number of single parents. Despite such realities, the Party continued to champion their traditional conception of a small family and provided interest-free loans (of 5000 Marks) to young newlyweds to finance their new lives together. The birth of every child reduced the amount to be repaid – the birth of three children annulled the loan altogether. Young mothers received a year's maternity leave paid at the same rate as sick leave. After the year, the state guaranteed a return to their job and the expanded provision of crèches, Kindergarten facilities and after-school childcare made this possibility a reality. The result was that over 90 % of children in the GDR were raised in collective units. Such provision was not without its darker side and many children felt

WOMEN IN MANAGEMENT POSITIONS, 1988

POLITICS
1 minister

INDUSTRY
2,4 % of state combine directors

UNIVERSITY
15 % of university lecturers

TRADES
20 % of master tradespersons

THE SOCIAL SERVICES
52 % of the group leaders

NET EARNINGS IN COMPARISON 1988

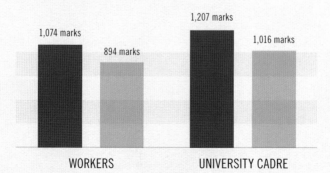

1,074 marks   894 marks   1,207 marks   1,016 marks

WORKERS   UNIVERSITY CADRE

unhappy in these state institutions. Should the child become ill, a parent (usually the mother) had to stay at home, making widespread absenteeism at work a common problem.

The system of crèche provision became a topic of controversy in reunited Germany and some even identified aspects of the system (such as the collective potty time) as contributory factors to what they recognized as an East German tendency towards the »authoritarian personality«. It is certain that East German society was strongly shaped by working mothers. Although their income secured women a high degree of independence, the role of the woman in the family remained a traditional one, and mothers retained their focus on cooking and child-rearing. Men were responsible for the car and other machinery. This was reflected in the workplace – state feminism did nothing to increase the number of women in management positions, which remained a male domain.

Left The kitchen in the exhibition

◼ CONSIDER YE WHO JOIN YOUR HANDS

Pre-marital sex was widely-accepted in the GDR and sex education began at the age of 11. Girls were issued with the »Planned Child Pill« free of charge from the age of 16, and those who forgot to take it had to make recourse to the »rubber fifties«: condoms called »Mondos« sold for 50 Pfennigs a piece.

Many married their first love, typically in their early twenties. The ceremony was held in the registry office and rarely in Church. Marriage had its advantages – the right to a flat and a generous marriage credit. This did not guarantee happiness: 2 out of 3 women marrying young were divorced after only 3 years.

HERR SCHNI
AND HIS NEW GERMANY

GDR citizens could not complain about a paucity of political coverage in the media. 39 newspapers, 2 television stations and a variety of programmes bored their audience rigid with verbatim reports of the various speeches held at every SED Party conference. Good comrades were well-informed comrades. Newspaper-reading was always a very dry activity; the stilted language, known as »Party Chinese« dulled the reading experience considerably. Political reports were often dictated by the central organ of the SED ›Neues Deutschland‹, right down to the way in which each text was to be punctuated. Oases of light relief in this desert of drudgery were provided by the literature and theatre pages or stories about local history. Nevertheless, the only real surprises were provided by the weather report and football results. Hard political facts were usually hidden under an ideological blanket of hollow phrases.

Those wanting reliable information quickly were forced to tune in to a Western station – these mouth pieces of the class enemy enjoyed a large audience throughout the GDR. East German television was popular for its entertainment and old films.

Monday night was film night, with an offering from the large stock of 1930s and 1940s films provided at eight o'clock. Known as the »Monday Evening Film«, they attracted a sizeable audience. The happy end was soon followed by the opening credits of the »Black Channel«. Hosted by Karl-Eduard von Schnitzler, it consisted of nothing more than a collection of clippings from West German television accompanied by a derisive commentary. In this way, GDR citizens acquired a new unit of time: »a Schni« which consisted of the length of time which it required to change channels as soon as Schnitzler introduced himself.

Politics aside, GDR entertainment television was popular, even in West Germany. Programmes such as Willi Schwabe's ›Rumpelkammer‹ and ›Ein Kessel Buntes‹ provided excitement, fun and a great deal of laughter. In short, everything that was missing from the ›Neues Deutschland‹.

TV TRANSMISSION
FROM THE FRG INTO THE TERRITORY OF THE GDR

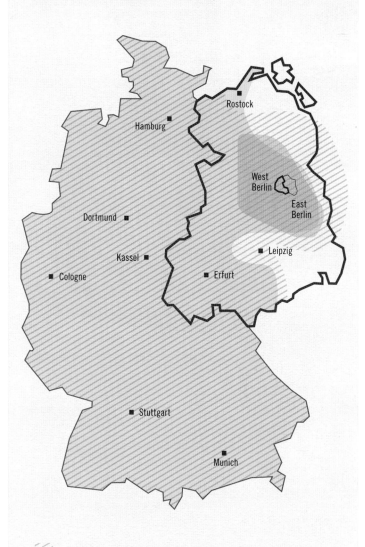

TRANSMISSION AREA OF THE FIRST (WEST) GERMAN TV CHANNEL

TRANSMISSION AREA OF THE SECOND (WEST) GERMAN TV CHANNEL

TRANSMISSION FROM WEST BERLIN

SOME TELEVISION PROGRAMMES

DER SCHWARZE KANAL

Unable to prevent its citizens from watching West German television, the authorities decided to make sure that everyone knew how
best to understand it. Karl-Eduard von Schnitzler, known more
popular as »Muck-Raker Eddy«, showed excerpts from West German television, adding his own derisive commentary.

AKTUELLE KAMERA

Scheduled conveniently at half-past seven, the GDR news bul-
letin fitted exactly between the two West German news broad-
casts, enabling the GDR citizens to get both sides of the story.

PRISMA

The political programme with the subtitle »Problems – Processes – People« examined questions from the economy, society and politics and drew attention to problems.

UNSER SANDMÄNNCHEN

Every evening at ten to seven saw the appearance of the Sand Man. A 25 cm puppet with a goatee beard and a jelly bag cap wished the children a good night and sent them off to bed. Popular in the GDR, the Sand Man still visits children today.

MACH MIT, MACH'S NACH, MACH'S BESSER

Every Sunday afternoon saw Gerhard »Adi« Adolph host a contest between two school classes in a number of sporting disciplines. The end of year saw the teams compete for a trophy from the National Olympic Committee.

The Autumn exhibition 1966, The International Fashion Show in the Kulturzentrum Südwest, Leipzig

Sybille's promise ↓

Die Verheißung der Sibylle

The Greek saga of Sybille tells of a woman able to predict the future. The most popular fashion magazine in the GDR was also called ›Sybille‹, but her predictions tended to be somewhat unrealistic. Showing modern, fashionable, state-of-the-art clothing, it ignored the reality of supply – such clothes existed nowhere in the GDR. The East German

fashion industry wanted both to distance itself from Western fashion and produce well-wearing and practical clothing suited to the needs of working women. Nevertheless, the »Berlin Fashion Institute« never succeeded in creating a new aesthetic and at best, managed to copy Western fashion. Hampered by the heavily bureaucratic planned economy, the East German fashion industry often found itself (or so it believed) designing a world-beating collection only to find that they could not produce the clothes fast enough. The supply of materials also dictated large-scale changes to their designs, reducing them to the aesthetic minimum. A new SED dictum from the

The Autumn fashion exhibition 1972 – »Youth 73«

1960s also influenced fashion: »Chemistry brings bread, prosperity and beauty«. The high price of cotton and the necessity of its import forced East German clothing manufacturers to depend on the use of artificial fibres. In the GDR, cars not dresses were made of cotton and the clothes were made of plastic. Uninspired, synthetic clothing of poor quality did not enthuse the fashion-conscious citizen. Those with West German relatives waited for gifts, those without made do and mended. At least ›Sybille‹ helped those ready to help themselves, providing a range of sewing patterns. She may have promised much, but it was the reader that had to deliver.

A LAND OF BIBLIOPHILES

Visitors from West Germany were often amazed by the sheer number of books occupying the restricted space in East German homes. Displayed on book-shelves re-functioned from spare wood, they often sagged under the weight of their learned contents. With books enjoying a high scarcity value, such libraries were the result of much time and patience.

Books from Eastern authors such as Christa Wolf or Stefan Heym were as difficult to find as those by their West

German counterparts Günter Grass and Heinrich Böll.

Indeed, the stories of their acquisition were often as complicated and interesting as those recounted between the pages. Good contacts to a book dealer were as valuable as an understanding with a car mechanic. Networks of bibliophiles spread rumours of small bookshops in tiny provincial villages, or the book trade within the National People's Army. They were also quick to congregate in bookshops, theatres and exhibitions to discuss Kafka, Rilke and Mann in a way entirely different to the Party functionaries or other practitioners of »doubleplusgood« thought. A casual reference to Orwell's Newspeak spoke volumes – indicating not just erudition, but a clear political stance. Subject to a strict ban, George Orwell's »1984« was available in only a few covert copies which were passed from hand to hand.

A number of intellectuals retreated into reading as many others retreated

to their summer homes. In some senses, this freedom of thought was no less an illusion than the rural idyll of an allotment. With his nose deep in a book, the reader could embark on the international travel that the SED denied him. With Dickens to London or with Zola to Paris, the possibilities were endless.

Debates of themes forbidden by the Party were held in plays, books and films – audiences lapped up every double entendre which the censor had missed. The »intellectual workers« were prized so highly because their work contrasted so strongly with the vacuity of the regime. A full bookcase thus acted as a barricade against the trivial nature of the SED state.

■ AN ANECDOTE

Book dealers gathered once a week to place their orders. The magnitude of the orders which they placed – often numbering between 20,000 and 50,000 copies – were far from realistic. They expected an order for 20,000 volumes to be answered with a delivery of 20 and exaggerated so as to ensure delivery of this paltry number.

Critical authors such as Christa Wolf or Stefan Heym were especially popular. Of 100,000 copies ordered, at least 5 would arrive, satisfying the demands of all the bookshop employees, but leaving little for the regular customers.

ESCAPE TO A PRIVATE IDYLL

The Socialist citizen was supposed to pass his free time in a »meaningful« fashion. »Meaningful« time usually implied time spent in the collective – hence the large number of »Houses of Culture«, youth clubs and sporting facilities built by the government so as to enable collective hobbies to thrive. Nevertheless, the urge to subject oneself to state propaganda after a hard day's indoctrination at work was always minimal at best. The legendary Houses of Culture, which sprang up like mushrooms in the 1950s, soon fell into neglect.

What then to do on a Saturday night under Socialism? Tickets for the theatre and cabaret were hard to come by and an evening in a restaurant involved a very long wait. Discos were often full to bursting, so television became very popular, as was reading. The most symbolic of past-times in the GDR was the retreat to one's Datsche or summer house. With a lot of love and even more effort, a large number of ordinary citizens built their very own holiday home. Indeed, it was this very effort, requiring a great deal of thought and individualism (two traits lacking from the major-

GARDEN GNOMES

24.5 %

Of East Germans preferred to
spend their holidays gardening

70 %

Spend their weekends in their
gardens in 1985

5 hours

The time spent gardening
per week

2.6 million

Summer houses with gardens

855,000

Allotments in East Germany

55 %

Of East Germans owned
a garden in 1985

10 marks

The monthly rent for
a garden property

ity of jobs) which made this so popular.
Finding the requisite material and then
building the homes became a joint
project involving friends, neighbours
and colleagues. Downing tools in the
evening, the day's exertions were
washed down with beer and sausages.
Initially uneasy at this mass retreat
into the private sphere, the Party soon
made its peace with such projects, as
they were inordinately preferable to a
dash to the West.

ROCKING FOR PEACE

The Party frowned on many things, but especially on Western music. Rock 'n' Roll and beat bands such as the Beatles incurred their particular ire. The worst aspect was the appearance of their followers: long-haired, short-skirted, loud and unkempt. Unkempt referred to the »riveted trousers«, i.e. Jeans and leather jackets. The consequences for such »layabouts« could be serious, results ranging from a compulsory haircut to a prison sentence or a spell working in the mines.

It was difficult to get hold of Western music and the Berlin Wall put an end to the slow trickle of the illegally imported records brought across by fans. One trick to get round this was to tape music from Western radio programmes. GDR radio stations and discos concentrated on playing East German music, forced as they were by legislation (known as the 60/40 directive) prescribing that 60 % of air time be dedicated to music from the Eastern bloc. The other 40 % could be Western music, but only if it had been published by an East German record company. The directive was difficult to circumvent as all playlists had to be submitted for approval. Deviation from the rule was subject to punishment. To liven up the evening, resourceful »Record Entertainers« (the abbreviation DJ was also frowned upon) often just played the prescribed 60 % at the beginning of the evening before arrival of their guests. This satisfied the state and made for a good party.

The end of the 1970s saw the development of an East German rock scene. Initially opposed by the state, the Stasi

Staatliche Spielerlaubnis

für Disko-Techniker

auf der Grundlage der Anordnungen 1 und 2 über Diskothekveranstaltungen vom 15. 8. 1973 und vom 24. 5. 1976 und der Anordnung über die Vergütung der Tätigkeit von nebenberuflich tätigen Amateurmusikern, Berufsmusikern und Kapellensängern vom 1. Okt. 1973, Anlage 1, Abs. 16

eventually restricted itself to monitoring and surveillance. GDR rock bands met with wild popularity: the ›Puhdys‹, ›Silly‹, ›City‹ or ›Karat‹ are just some of the most well-known names. Some musicians were even allowed to give concerts and sell their records in West Germany – the state needed the foreign cash. The bands enjoyed some success in the Capitalist West: the LP ›Am Fenster‹ by ›City‹ went gold in West Germany and Greece and Peter Maffay's interpretation of the song ›Über sieben Brücken‹ (Over Seven Bridges) from ›Karat‹ made the song a hit in East and West alike.

Not every guitar-playing singer was allowed to earn a living with his talent. Aspiring rockers had to audition in front of a state commission to receive a license to play. Professional musicians required training, a university degree and a clean vest. Punk bands for instance were unlikely to receive official approval, as their appearance and anarchism were irreconcilable with SED cultural ideas. Bans on performing in public forced bands such as ›Schleimkeim‹, ›Planlos‹ and ›Müllstation‹ to perform in cellars, domestic courtyards and church premises. With Stasi informants at many such concerts, they were often brought to an abrupt end by a raid and a number of arrests.

Above Rock for peace, 1986; The International Tour for Peace,1983. *Centre* The »Puhdys«
Below Dean Reed, »the Red Elvis«; Guitarist from the band »City«

» I AM CONVINCED **COMRADES**, THAT WE SHOULD PUT A END **TO THE MONOTONY** OF THIS **YEAH, YEAH, YEAH** AND WHATEVER ELSE **IT IS THEY CHANT.«**

WALTER ULBRICHT

EVERY MAN EVERYWHERE – SPORT ONCE A WEEK

WALTER ULBRICHT

The GDR was a sporting nation. Not only was its practice anchored in the constitution, companies were obliged to provide sporting activities and schools provided both an obligatory and voluntary programme of sporting activity. Football, cycling, athletics and other (predominantly Olympic) disciplines were provided to make the population healthy and (more importantly) the nation successful. The SED hoped that success in international competitions would bring international respect and prestige, and in turn make the citizens of the GDR proud and happy.

The German Gymnastics and Sporting League (DTSB) visited kindergartens to recruit young talent and find them a place at a special sport school. The plan worked and established the GDR as one of the most successful sporting nations in the world.

The ice dancer Katarina Witt, the cyclist »Täve« Schur and the athlete Heike Drechsler soon advanced to international fame. Established as »Socialist role models« in the GDR, they were never referred to as »stars« as the word was far too English.

Apart from the prestige and hero status, the athletes had little to show for their success — a little more money, a new flat, their car was delivered earlier and they received the odd trip to Cuba. Very little in comparison to the commercial success enjoyed by their Western rivals. As a result, many were forced to continue working in their original jobs.

The most prestigious international result for the SED was the victory of their football team over West Germany. The two football teams met only once — the last game of the group stage of the 1974 Football World Cup. The game in Hamburg finished 1:0 to East Germany. The goal, scored by a now famous Jürgen Sparwasser, was heralded as a »victory over Capitalism«. Nevertheless, many East Germans had secretly supported their opponents.

Despite all this success, the Party remained insecure and resorted to other, more covert means to ensure success. Many athletes were doped, sometimes with, sometimes without their knowledge.

IHR PUNKT-
PROGRAMM
FÜRS
GANZE JAHR

SPORT HURTS

Copious amounts of Oral-Turinabol were administered to professional sportsmen and women from the 1970s. The anabolic steroid strengthens muscles and raises levels of aggression and risk-taking. Trainers even gave the drugs to children, passing them off as vitamins. Such »treatment« brings the risk of dangerous side-effects for the liver and hormone balance. Many athletes suffered considerable lasting damage. Others died.

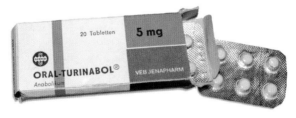

The swimmer four-times Olympic champion Roland Matthes

THE SUMMER GAMES

YEAR	LOCATION	GOLD	SILVER	BRONZE	RANK
1968	Mexico	9	9	7	5
1972	Munich	20	23	23	3
1976	Montréal	40	25	25	2
1980	Moscow	47	37	42	2
1984	Los Angeles	[boycotted by the GDR]			
1988	Seoul	37	35	30	2

Athlete and double Olympic champion Heike Drechsler

THE WINTER GAMES

YEAR	LOCATION	GOLD	SILVER	BRONZE	RANK
1968	Grenoble	1	2	2	10
1972	Sapporo	4	3	7	2
1976	Innsbruck	7	5	7	2
1980	Lake Placid	9	7	7	2
1984	Sarajevo	9	9	6	1
1988	Calgary	9	10	6	2

HOLIDAY DESTINATIONS ISSUED TO GDR CITITZENS IN 1988

ČSSR	**651 630**
USSR	**228 304**
Hungary	**109 637**
Bulgaria	**63 548**
Poland	**40 462**
Yugoslavia	**4 193**
Cuba	**1 283**
Finland	**1 010**

NORWAY

DENMA

THE NETHERLANDS

FRG

BELGIUM

LUXEMBUR

FRANCE

SWITZER

SPAIN

PORTUGAL

CUBA

1 283

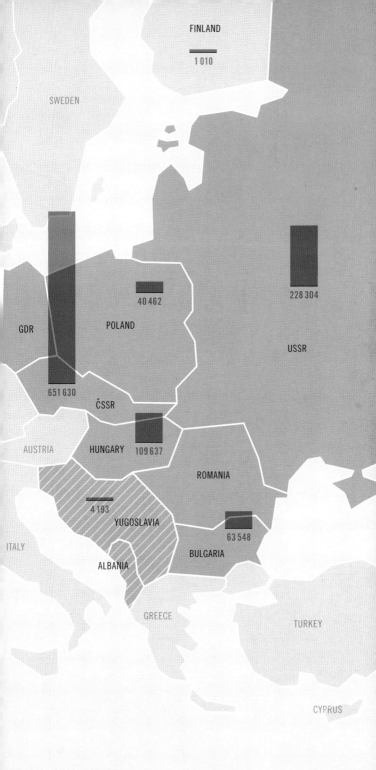

FINLAND
1 010

SWEDEN

POLAND
40 462

GDR

228 304

USSR

651 630

ČSSR

AUSTRIA

HUNGARY
109 637

ROMANIA

YUGOSLAVIA
4 193

ITALY

ALBANIA

BULGARIA
63 548

GREECE

TURKEY

CYPRUS

ONLY FLYING WOULD BE BETTER

Many GDR citizens dreamt of holidaying on a Mediterranean beach, but in vain. Even those business men, artists and scientists permitted to travel to Western countries for professional reasons were not allowed to take their family on holiday in the »Non-Socialist Currency Area«.

A typical summer holiday began in February with an application to the Travel Department of the Free German Trade Union Federation (FDGB), the largest provider of holidays in the GDR. Unbeatably good value, the packages they provided even included heavily re-duced train tickets to get there. Nevertheless, the dream tickets to the Baltic Sea were so scarce that would-be holiday-makers needed good contacts or a large portion of luck to obtain them. The same applied to holiday accommodation in Thuringia and to winter holidays in the Harz Mountains. Even those managing to get away were faced with a modest standard of comfort: communal bathrooms and meals were standard.

Company-owned holiday homes often provided a greater level of comfort, but at the cost of going on holiday with one's colleagues. The relaxation of

border controls after 1972 meant that the penniless young could hitch-hike to Warsaw or Prague, both countries providing a little more freedom and glamour. Even more circumvented the difficulties of mass provision and pitched their tent in the more beautiful areas of the GDR.

Others went even further, investigating the Black Sea Coast, Lake Balaton or the High Tatras – adventures which were difficult to book and very expensive. Once arrived, holiday-makers experienced numerous hurdles to any level of comfort – the GDR Mark was not an attractive currency and hoteliers responded by issuing table cloths and other luxuries to those paying in harder currencies.

POLITICS WITHOUT SWIMMING TRUNKS

The SED was displeased, but naturists got their way. Starting as a protest movement, the Free Body Culture (FKK) or naturism movement soon attracted a mass following. Four out of five East German regularly went swimming naked and only every tenth sun worshipper was opposed in principle to this more open form of relaxation. Failing in its attempts to outlaw naked swimming, the SED changed tack and appealed to its comrades to »spare the eyes of the nation« as the Minister for Culture Johannes R. Becher put it. The success of the ›FKK‹ movement was less the result of desire for greater sexual liberality than a desire to do something forbidden. Just once. Moreover, many Communists saw nakedness as an expression of true classlessness. With the »textile beaches« of the Mediterranean beyond the reach of East Germans citizens, they transformed GDR beaches into virtually swimwear-free zones.

Picture A normal day on the beach. Diorama in the exhibition.

»THE PARTY IS ALWAYS RIGHT«

III. SED Party Conference in Berlin, 1950

Finding the »Song of the Party« on the internet, many modern listeners cannot believe their ears. »I almost wet myself laughing« or »you're having me on« are just some of the comments. Far from a modern joke, the song, beginning with the (entirely serious) line »The Party, The Party, The Party is always right« was the official hymn of the SED from 1951.

Later, the Party tried to ignore its confident anthem yet without ever abandoning its claim to infallibility. The source of embarrassment was not the first line, but a later verse — »emerging from Lenin's spirit and hardened by Stalin – the Party, the Party, the Party.« Since his official debunking in 1956, Stalin was no longer heralded as the »Father of the Peoples« but a criminal who had betrayed the revolution. His name could no longer be mentioned. Loading all guilt squarely on the shoulders of this convenient Soviet scapegoat, the SED refused to countenance the possibility that it had any hand in the litany of failure and error of which Stalin was accused. To this end, the SED was forced to rewrite its own history.

After Walter Ulbricht's (forced) retirement in 1971, he disappeared from public view almost entirely. Despite changing course in a number of spheres, Ulbricht's successor Erich Honecker still forbade any discussions of error. With its power sacrosanct and its lead-

TIMELINE SED

1945

The ban on the Communist Party of Germany (KPD) and the Social Democratic Party of Germany (SPD) is lifted in the Soviet zone of occupation

1946

The forced union of the KPD and SPD to form the Socialist Unity Party of Germany (SED)

1948

The transformation of the SED into a Stalinist cadre party

1953

The death of Stalin and announcement of the New Course. The People's Uprising on 17 June

1956

XX. Party Conference of the Soviet Communist Party begins de-Stalinization

1963

VI. Party Conference. Announcement of the New Economic System of Planning and Management

1971

The transfer of power from Walter Ulbricht to Erich Honecker. The VIII. Party Conference announces the Unity of Social and Economic Policy

1985

Gorbachev begins his reforms in the Soviet Union

1989

The Party loses power and renames itself as the Party of Democratic Socialism (PDS)

1990

ing role anchored in the first paragraph of the GDR constitution, the SED maintained iron discipline amongst its 2.3 million members. Any deviation from the official line met with immediate odium and expulsion from the ranks of the political avant guarde.

The Party stood by its leadership even after it became clear that the final crisis of Socialism was upon them. There was much internal debate about the wisdom of Honecker's inflexible rejection of Soviet reforms, but practised in loyalty, the membership was unable to

effect any opposition. The claim to infallibility by the Party leadership had
stifled all independent thought. The
Party marched to their ruin with their
eyes wide open.

Erich Honecker congratulates
Walter Ulbricht at his birthday celebrations
(Berlin 1973)

FATHER STATE

As every school child was taught, »the State is the instrument of the ruling class.« This formula was a good reflection of reality. The state was the instrument of power of the ruling Party, inextricably linked but not identical with it. The apparatus of the state was controlled by the Party, but it was more than the Party. In essence, state and society were identical. The theory of the separation of the powers – legislation, administration and justice being controlled by separate branches – had been established as a key feature of bourgeois society since the eighteenth century.

In Socialism however, the magic word was unity and the state interfered in almost every area of life. As the most senior economic planner, the state regulated even the smallest step taken in production, trade and commerce. The state was supreme in schools, universities, art and culture. State institutions were responsible for allocating housing, kindergarten places, automobiles and telephones. Yet the state was more than a mere administrator. Asserting a clear claim to national education, the state cast itself in the role of a strict Father who punished and rewarded his children. Being good and loving the Father could bring much reward, but never any rights. The GDR lacked all administrative jurisdiction and no constitutional

court. Appeals were senseless – the courts were part of the state. The citizen's only hope was to file a petition to various state organs, commercial organizations, offices and administrations or even to the newspapers and television.

The organs of the state (the GDR spoke of its state as though it were a living organism) liked to appear benevolent, as the parlous state of its economy made the SED sensitive to public happiness. Sometimes, they were even understanding and now and again reacted in an unbureaucratic manner.

An instruction from the top was simply enforced and the legal niceties were ironed out afterwards. Bad children were disciplined harshly, and Father never hesitated to reach for his belt.

The security organs – Police, the Courts and Stasi – were all part of the state which would never have functioned without the threat of force.

THE REINS OF POWER

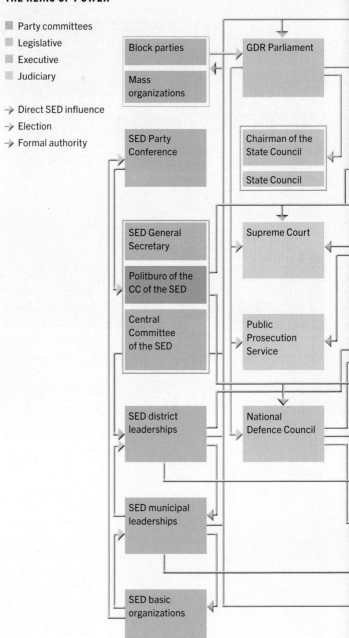

- Party committees
- Legislative
- Executive
- Judiciary

→ Direct SED influence
→ Election
→ Formal authority

Block parties

Mass organizations

GDR Parliament

SED Party Conference

Chairman of the State Council

State Council

SED General Secretary

Politburo of the CC of the SED

Central Committee of the SED

Supreme Court

Public Prosecution Service

SED district leaderships

National Defence Council

SED municipal leaderships

SED basic organizations

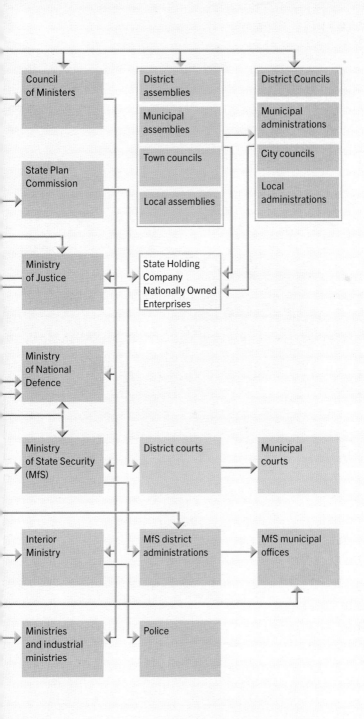

17. MAI WAHLTA

Klare Perspektive für Handwerkerfleiß

UNSERE STIM den Kandidaten der National Front!

»GOING FOLDING«

The whole rotten business was uncovered on 7 May 1989 and long-held suspicions finally became a certainty. The fantastic results achieved by the state after every election were the result of manipulation. Where pressure, propaganda and the lack of alternatives failed, the SED leadership simply cheated and published incorrect figures.

Observing the proceedings on the 7 May, members of Church groupings proved that the electorate had been systematically deceived. Judging by appearances, Polling Day on 7 May was like any other. State propaganda pulled out all the stops. Wearing their Sunday best, happy people carried placards bearing »GDR — My Fatherland« and billboards exhorted passers-by to support the National Front. Polling stations were flanked by Students in FDJ blue and flag-waving children. NVA units marched-off together to cast their vote. Those staying at home received a visit from officials, reminding them of their duty to vote.

Amidst this close observance of the old rituals, there were small differences. The proportion of people using the polling booths was considerably higher than previous years, when the folded ballot paper was cast in the urn directly after its issue. Going to the booth was a dangerous and brave act. Despite official claims to the contrary, elections were not free, the ballot was not secret and the systems were not transparent.

The act of voting was popularly referred to as »going folding« – little more was required. The lists of the National Front were filled with the nominations of the SED. There were no boxes to make any crosses and rejection was not really part of the plan. A »no« vote required the citizen to cross through every single name on the list. All those taking the brave step of using the polling booth (located in the furthest corner of the room) had first to pass the massed ranks of election officials, who would suspect them of being subversive enemy elements.

Shortly before the closure of the Polling Stations on the evening of 7 May, a number of people suddenly arrived to observe the proceedings. Checking the count, they registered up to 20 % »no« votes in some Polling Stations. This was not reflected in the official return of 98.85 »yes« votes. Going public with their findings, civil rights activists organized protests on the Alexanderplatz on every 7th day of the following months. That of 7 October 1989 sparked a course of events ending in the Peaceful Revolution.

NEUES

ORGAN DES ZENTRALK(

Eindrucksvolles

98,85 P

Kandid

12 182 050 Bürger gaben in Gemei
Stimmrecht wahr / Arbeitskolle

Vorsitzender der Wahlkommission gab vorläufiges Wahlergebnis bekannt

Berlin (ADN). Der Vorsitzende der Wahlkommission der Republik, Egon Krenz, Mitglied des Politbüros und Sekretär des Zentralkomitees der SED, gab am Abend des 7. Mai 1989 im Fernsehen der DDR das vorläufige Gesamtergebnis der Wahlen bekannt:

Liebe Bürgerinnen und Bürger der Deutschen Demokratischen Republik!

Liebe Freunde und Genossen!

Die Kommunalwahlen im 40. Jahr unseres Arbeiter-und-Bauern-Staates wurden zu einem eindrucksvollen Votum für die Kandidaten der Nationalen Front der Deutschen Demokratischen Republik. Das vorläufige zusammengefaßte Gesamtergebnis der Wahlen zu den Stadtbezirksversammlungen von Berlin, zu den Kreistagen und den Stadtverordnetenversammlungen der Stadtkreise widerspiegelt das Bekenntnis der Wählerinnen und Wähler zu den Zielen des gemeinsamen Wahlprogramms, für das weitere Gedenken unserer Städte und Gemeinden, für einen starken Sozialismus und einen sicheren Frieden.

Wahlberechtigt waren 12 488 742 Bürger.

Es wurden 12 335 487 Stimmen abgegeben.

Das entspricht einer Wahlbeteiligung von 98,77 Prozent.

Die Zahl der gültigen Stimmen beträgt 12 324 351.

Das sind 99,91 Prozent.

Die Zahl der ungültigen Stimmen beträgt 11 138.

Das sind 0,09 Prozent.

Für die Wahlvorschläge der

Nationalen Front
schen Demokratis
blik wurden 12 18:
Stimmen abgegeber

Das sind 98,85 Pr
Gegen die Wa
wurden 142 301 S
gegeben.

Das sind 1,15 Pro:

Im Namen der
mission der Republ
allen, die durch il
lichen Einsatz zur
chen Verlauf der
wahlen beigetra
Dank gilt den mel
Bürgern, die in de
missionen tätig
über 235 000 Mit
den Wahlvorstän
über 1 Million Wa
den Kreisen, Städt
meinden.

Herzlich gratulie
neugewählten A
und Nachfolgekan
das Vertrauen der
hielten. Von ihrem
tungsbewußtsein, il
und Können, von
trauensvollen Kont
Bürgern hängt we
Erfolg unserer
politik ab. Für ih.
netentätigkeit zum
unserer Städte und
zur Stärkung uns
stischen Vaterlande
schen Demokratis
blik, wünsche ich
vertretern der Bevö

»Gehen wir mit
auf den XII. Pa
Sozialistischen E
Deutschlands im fo
nis aller Klasser
ten weiter voran
des Volkes und
des Friedens.

UdSSR und DDR verbi
**brüderliche Freundsc
und gemeinsame Ide**

Grußadresse der Partei- und Staats
der UdSSR zum 44. Jahrestag der B
des deutschen Volkes vom Faschist

Generalsekretär
des Zentralkomitees der
Sozialistischen
Einheitspartei Deutschlands
und Vorsitzenden
des Staatsrates der
Deutschen Demokratischen
Republik
Genossen Erich Honecker

Vorsitzenden des Ministerrates
der Deutschen Demokratischen
Republik
Genossen Willi Stoph

Liebe Genossen!
Anläßlich des 44. Jahrestages
der Befreiung des deutschen
Volkes vom Faschismus übermitteln wir Ihnen, dem Zentralkomitee der Sozialistischen Einheitspartei Deutschlands, dem Staatsrat und dem Ministerrat, allen Bürgern der Deutschen Demokratischen Republik herzliche Glückwünsche und freundschaftliche Grüße.

Mit dem Tag des großen Sieges über den Hitlerfaschismus begann eine neue Zeitrechnung. Auf deutscher Erde trafen die

die für die politische
Befreiung der arbei
schen gekämpft hal
Hochgeschätzt we
Sowjetunion die
der brüderlichen
der internationaler
und gegenseitig ver
zusammenarbeit, die
und SED, die Völker
der fest verbinden.
wirklichung der Au
gegenwärtigen wich
des sozialistischen
Übereinstimmung n
nalen Erfordernis:
die UdSSR und
einem Ziel, lassen
gemeinsamen Ide
Dabei bemühen s
mächtige Potential
len Zusammenarbei
des Sozialismus, e
zung des neuen pol
kens in den interna
gelegenheiten imm
ger zu erschließen,
effektiver zu nutzen
Wir wünschen Ihn
nossen, den Komm
deller Bürgern der

Proletarier aller Länder, vereinigt euch!

Montag,
8. Mai 1989
44. Jahrgang / Nr. 107

B-Ausgabe
Einzelpreis 15 Pf

Redaktion und Verlag: Franz-Mehring-Platz 1, Berlin, 1017, Telefon: 5 83 10 (Sammelnummer). Abonnementspreis monatlich 3,50 Mark. ISSN 0323–3049

DEUTSCHLAND

DER SOZIALISTISCHEN EINHEITSPARTEI DEUTSCHLANDS

...nis zu unserer Politik des Friedens und des Sozialismus

...zent stimmten für die
...en der Nationalen Front

...en und Kreisen den Volksvertretern ihr Vertrauen / Hohe Wahlbeteiligung: 98,77 Prozent nahmen ihr ... mit erfüllten und überbotenen Plänen / Neue Initiativen im Wettbewerb zum 40. Jahrestag der DDR

Vorläufiges Ergebnis der Wahlen am 7. Mai 1989
zu den Stadtbezirksversammlungen von Berlin, Hauptstadt der DDR,
zu den Kreistagen und den Stadtverordnetenversammlungen der Stadtkreise

	Wahlberechtigte insgesamt	Abgegebene Stimmen insgesamt	Wahlbeteiligung in %	UNGÜLTIGE STIMMEN absolut	in %	GÜLTIGE STIMMEN insgesamt absolut	in %	GÜLTIGE STIMMEN für den Wahlvorschlag absolut	in %	GÜLTIGE STIMMEN Gegen den Wahlvorschlag absolut	in %
DDR	12 488 762	12 335 487	98,77	11 136	0,09	12 324 351	99,91	12 182 050	98,85	142 301	1,15
Bezirk											
Berlin, Hauptstadt der DDR	972 178	944 923	97,20	708	0,07	944 215	99,93	931 250	98,63	12 965	1,37
Cottbus	644 415	637 245	98,89	592	0,09	636 653	99,91	632 803	99,40	3 850	0,60
Dresden	1 321 857	1 296 986	98,12	1 833	0,14	1 295 153	99,86	1 269 950	98,05	25 203	1,95
Erfurt	928 281	924 018	99,54	673	0,07	923 345	99,93	918 531	99,48	4 814	0,52
Frankfurt	518 696	514 806	99,25	344	0,07	514 462	99,93	503 914	97,95	10 548	2,05
Gera	559 412	552 084	99,38	577	0,10	552 407	99,90	546 809	98,99	5 598	1,01
Halle	1 236 614	1 226 982	99,28	621	0,05	1 226 361	99,95	1 217 979	99,37	8 382	0,63
Karl-Marx-Stadt	1 419 289	1 392 299	98,10	1 525	0,11	1 390 774	99,89	1 368 258	98,38	22 516	1,62
Leipzig	1 020 440	1 007 086	98,69	725	0,07	1 006 361	99,85	982 864	97,67	23 497	2,33
Magdeburg	937 264	925 012	98,69	373	0,04	924 639	99,96	918 554	99,34	6 085	0,66
Neubrandenburg	452 580	449 221	99,21	157	0,03	449 144	99,97	446 290	99,36	2 874	0,64
Potsdam	843 361	839 317	99,52	1 659	0,22	837 458	99,78	831 216	99,25	6 242	0,75
Rostock	677 239	671 244	99,11	545	0,08	670 699	99,92	667 352	99,50	3 347	0,50
Schwerin	440 062	435 683	99,00	227	0,05	435 456	99,95	432 409	99,33	3 047	0,70
Suhl	419 765	417 581	99,48	277	0,09	417 204	99,91	413 871	99,20	3 333	0,80

...h Honecker, Willi Stoph, Horst Sindermann und ihre Ehefrauen gaben ihre Stimme im Wahllokal Berlin-Niederschönhausen ab   Foto: ND-Murza

PLAYING AT PARLIAMENT

No one provided a better summary of Communist policy in May 1945 than Walter Ulbricht. Faced by considerable impatience from his comrades at the need to share power with bourgeois and Christian Democratic parties he replied: »it has to look democratic but we've got to have everything under our control.«

In addition to the working class parties of the KPD (Communist Party of Germany) and SPD (Social Democratic Party of Germany) the CDU (Christian Democratic Union of Germany) and the Liberal Democratic Party of Germany (LDP, later renamed as the LDPD) were also licensed as political parties. Initially given considerable room for manoeuvre, the freedoms of the bourgeois parties were curtailed in 1947/8.

The CDU, LDP and the subsequently founded National Democratic Party of Germany (NDPD) and the Democratic Peasants Party of Germany (DBD) were later forced to join the organizational straitjacket of the National Front. The parties of the democratic bloc – hence their name the »bloc parties« – were now firmly integrated into the SED sys-

MEMBERSHIP OF THE BLOC PARTIES (1987)

110,000 NDPD

140,000 CDU

117,000 DBD

106,000 LDPD

An NVA formation enters the CDU Party Conference in Dresden 1985

tem of rule. These organizations catered for all tastes – former Nazis and officers found a welcome in the NDPD; artisans and businessmen were integrated into the LDPD and independent farmers came to the DBD.

Christianity was difficult to integrate. Despite the irreconcilable claims of Christianity and Marxist Leninism, the SED wanted Christians to work with them in the establishment of the GDR.

The bloc parties were given equal representation in the GDR Parliament, the State Council and the district and municipal assemblies. Raising their hands dutifully to every proposal made by the SED, the parties even voted against the interests of their own members and in 1972, the LDPD gave its approval to the expropriation of the remnants of private industry. Given functions in the cultural sphere, the co-operation of CDU representatives appeared to indicate the reconciliation of Marxism and Christianity. No one noticed that Christian children were systematically denied access to further and higher education.

Those wanting to make a career often saw membership of one of the bloc parties as the lesser of two evils. As a result, the bloc parties were often despised by both sides – by the general public for their opportunism and obsequiousness and by the SED for their potential unreliability. For their part, the members of these parties felt they had the opportunity to effect positive change within their immediate environments, without the need for (in their eyes futile) confrontation with the authorities. Nevertheless, the price for this choice was a public and unambiguous commitment to the GDR and Socialism.

WORKERS' RIGHTS IN THE WORKERS' PARADISE

In capitalism, the unions acted to represent the interests of the workers, conducting industrial disputes and wage negotiations and organizing demonstrations and strikes. None of this existed in the GDR. There was no need – the happiness of the workers was a key aspect of the »Worker's and Peasant's State.« All factories were »owned by the people« and there was no »exploitation« to fight. With class war consigned to the history books, the functionaries of the Free German Trade Union Federation were better known for their prodigious capacity for sleepiness than their exercise of power.

Nevertheless, they did hold a few trumps in their hand. One was the system of bonus payments payable to model workers – the factory union leadership put forward a name to the state factory manager. The FDGB also had influence in the »End of Year Bonus«, a sort of thirteenth month's salary. Apart from this, the FDGB held responsibility for the cultural edification of its members, organizing a great deal of amateur dramatics, folk singing and the like, the result of which could be admired at the regular »Workers' Festivals.« Football fans were more interested in the annual FDGB cup.

The the main focus of the FDGB's activities was its holiday provision. Maintaining a large number of holiday homes from the Baltic Sea to the Erz Mountains, the FDGB travel agency was the largest tourist provider in the GDR.

In addition to such land-locked activities, FDGB holiday cruisers such as the ›Fritz Heckert‹ or ›Völkerfreundschaft‹ (peace between peoples) steamed the high seas. Normal citizens never came anywhere near such luxury, as the regime was always afraid that they would take the opportunity to effect their escape. The average experience of an FDGB holiday was 14 days full board in a ramshackle holiday home in Thuringia. Mass tourism with poor service, mass catering and lights out at 11 was all that holiday-makers could expect. Despite the basic nature of the facilities, such holidays had the advantage that they were easily affordable for a five-person family. What the majority of holiday-makers did not know was that most of the holiday homes were private properties expropriated by the SED in the early 1950s.

By the end of the 1980s, the FDGB had advanced to a membership of around 9.5 million workers; a figure representing the great majority of the workforce. The dissolution of the union upon reunification meant that it was not there when its former members needed protection against serious curtailments of their rights.

Left The FDGB holiday home
»Schöne Aussicht«, at Schmiedefeld
Middle The FDGB holiday home
»Ringberghaus« at Suhl
Right The FDGB cruise ship »MS Fritz Heckert«

FROM THE »I« TO THE »WE«

The collective is more important than the individual. SED functionaries never tired of celebrating the victory of the »we« over the »I.« Their main concern was with mass groups such as children, women and workers, which they sought to organize and control. Presiding over all these conglomerations was the Party, which organized choirs to celebrate it as the »Mother of the Masses.«

According to the SED propaganda, the life of the »class enemy« in the West was characterized by egoism, loneliness and social indifference. Comrades in the GDR on the other hand enjoyed solidarity and public spirit. How willing a person was to accept and enjoy the advantages provided by the Socialist community became clear in school. The first indication was membership in the Pioneers and the Free German Youth (FDJ), a loyalty test which the majority passed with flying colours. There were always two or three in the class who refused, but it was clear that they ran the risk of discrimination in their later career. The rest of the class took part, most out of a sense of duty and with marginal interest, some with real enthusiasm. The FDJ provided them with camping trips, choirs and poetry seminars. As the only officially permitted youth organization, it was charged with the task of forming the youth in its care into »class-conscious Socialists«, a task in which it experienced only moderate success.

The mass organizations gave the GDR a vaguely democratic appearance. All FDJ members (complete with blue shirt and a golden motif of the rising sun on the left arm) were eligible for and could vote in the elections for the more minor offices. Many did so and some became treasurer, secretary or group leader. Holding such offices in the FDJ, otherwise known as the »fighting reserve of the Party« was good for the career.

Living proof of this assumption was Erich Honecker – for many years the chairman of the FDJ, he finished his career as the Head of the GDR.

Having left the FDJ, adults did not lack opportunities to collect membership books, badges and emblems. Those not wishing to join the SED or one of the bloc parties could enter the Free German Trade Union Federation (FDGB) or the Democratic Women's League of Germany (DFD), leap around in the German Gymnastics and Sporting League (DTSB), or join the Allotment and Small Animal Breeding Association (VKSK) or the Society for German–Soviet Friendship (DSF).

Indeed, it was more common to find someone wearing swimming trunks on a nudist's beach than it was to meet someone not in at least one of these groupings. Nevertheless, the »social activity« of the majority of group members was limited to payment of the membership fee. Above all, the mass organizations served to mitigate the suspicion of the authorities.

»SOVIET SOLDIERS, WE THANK YOU«

Popping the champagne corks on 7 November 1967, the group gathered in the Soviet embassy on East Berlin's Unter den Linden celebrated the fiftieth anniversary of the »Great Socialist October Revolution.«

The marathon of celebrations involving military displays, pathos-laden speeches, monumental concerts and dance festivals was rounded-off with a spectacular celebratory banquet. This orgy of spectacle matched the size of the claim – the founding myth of a world empire. The Socialist brother states from Cuba to North Korea all sent telegrams, gifts and delegations to Moscow to congratulate their big brother.

Not wanting to be outdone, the GDR organized a series of lectures, films and books. The bosses of the Academy of Arts and the state record company VEB Deutsche Schallplatten even managed to convince the egocentric singer Ernst Busch (better known as the »Red Orpheus«) to produce a German-Soviet song cycle. The resulting record with a John Heartfield cover was presented before a live television audience to a Soviet delegation in East Germany at a ceremony held in Berlin. The presentation was accompanied by a performance from the sexagenarian Busch, whose rendition of the songs moved his Soviet guests to tears. The more sober response of the GDR television audience reflected their true feelings towards the international Socialist brotherhood, amounting as it did, to a forced union.

Even the large membership of the Society for German-Soviet Friendship (DSF) could not hide the latent scepticism towards all things Russian. With a subscription of only a few pfennigs, this Society allowed a number of people to demonstrate the expected »social engagement« at no great cost whilst leaving maintenance of the much-lauded »steadfast friendship with the Soviet Union« to the Socialist patriarchs such as Ernst Busch.

Learning of the Stalinist crimes during his Moscow exile 1935–1937, the actor and singer maintained a steadfast silence about the darker side of Communism throughout his entire life. Such silence did little however to diminish the poor image of the USSR. Far from a friend, the ›Russe‹ was seen exclusively as an occupier and the compulsory Russian as the first foreign language in schools was never popular. Knowledge of the language was of little value, even on holidays in the other brother states, as Russian was even more unpopular in the rest of the Eastern bloc.

The situation changed only after the rise of Michael Gorbachev in 1985. Intrigued by Glasnost and Perestroika, many in the GDR tried frantically to

Picture The Soviet War Memorial, Berlin-Treptow

brush up their Russian in order to be able to read Pravda in the original. Membership of the DSF suddenly assumed a subversive character and readings from Russian authors, Russian film presentations and art exhibitions all began to incur SED suspicion.

A CENTIMETRE
A DAY
AND THEN
I'M AWAY

They tried everything, even getting blind drunk the night before the medical. Yet nothing helped. Balance problems, pale skin, even short-term blindness did not prevent classification as »fully fit for service in the National People's Army.« After the usual diagnosis of flat and splay feet, a bent spine and slight deafness, the recruit was then sent directly to the recruiting board where the decision was made as to the length of service – the minimum of 18 months or a full three years. Some were even »persuaded« to enrol as a professional non-commissioned or commissioned officer.

A whole range of enticement and threats were employed to extract a »voluntary commitment« to a life in the army. The recruit was faced with a difficult task – that of refusing extra service yet retaining his appearance as a committed Socialist.

Candidates for the Border Guard Division were also given a grilling. »Your uncle lives in West Germany. If you were to meet him on the border within the scope of imperialist aggression, would you hesitate in shooting?« The candidate pauses. »Both my schooling and my membership of the young pioneers have formed me into a peace-loving person. I cannot even begin to think that I could shoot at anyone.« That was the wrong answer. With a crimson face, the Major bellows his response: »GET OUT!« Not bad. At least the recruit avoids serving on the border.

The conscription order came by post. Outlining the time and place of registration, it also specified what to bring: a bar of soap, shaving and sewing kit, cutlery, shoe cleaning equipment and toothpaste – all in duplicate. After collecting these items, the potential recruit had a hair cut and bid his fond farewells. The next 18 months (or even three years) now consisted of marching, standing to attention, training and military cleanliness, interspersed with drunken singing and political instruction.

Returning to his family and friends for leave, the young soldier surprised those who knew him with the foreign jargon of soldiery. The most important thing he had to do on leave was to buy a tape measure. Back at the barracks, he cut off a centimetre a day, and on this covert calendar, counted the days until his service ended.

CONSTRUCTION SOLDIERS

Since 1964, national servicemen in the GDR were given the choice between military service and serving in a construction battalion. Despite suffering considerable educational and professional discrimination, 27,000 young men chose to follow their conscience and served as so-called »construction soldiers« until 1989.

NUMBER OF CONSTRUCTION SOLDIERS
DRAFTED INTO THE NVA

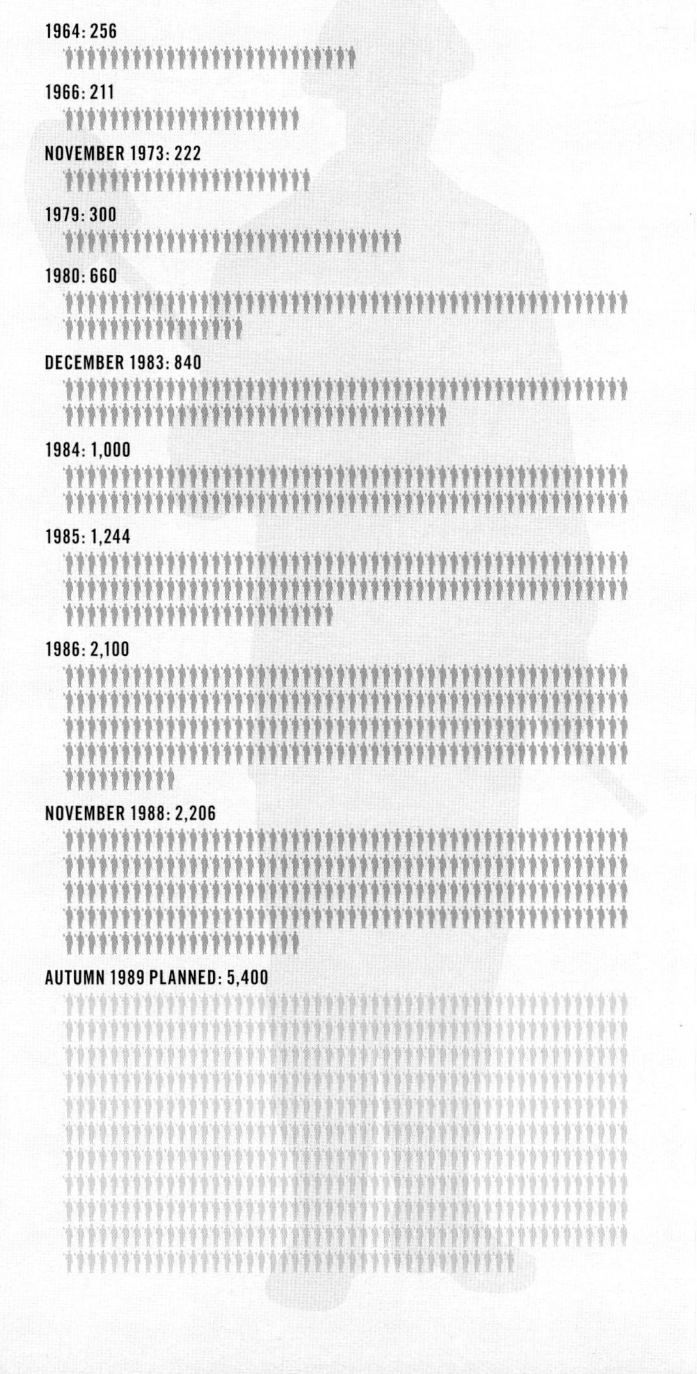

1964: 256

1966: 211

NOVEMBER 1973: 222

1979: 300

1980: 660

DECEMBER 1983: 840

1984: 1,000

1985: 1,244

1986: 2,100

NOVEMBER 1988: 2,206

AUTUMN 1989 PLANNED: 5,400

WHO IS LISTENING?

Every single East German had to live with the possibility that their post was being opened, their telephone and flat were bugged and that someone was spying on them. They had no right of appeal against the actions of the Stasi. Enjoying unrestricted access to all documents ranging from bank statements to medical records, the Stasi could employ perfidious methods known as »disruption« to destroy not only the professional but also the family lives of individuals.

One of the measures taken by the GDR immediately after its foundation in 1949 was to establish the Ministry for State Security in 1950. The Stasi was the secret police, ideological watchdog, foreign intelligence agency and enforcement agency all rolled into one with its own military units, a network of remand prisons, safe houses and other buildings, its own health service, utility and leisure facilities, special communications systems and an internationally active economic empire. Despite this impressive level of organization and range of activities, the Stasi was never a »state within a state«, but the very mechanism holding the SED state together. Calling itself the »shield and sword of the Party«, the Stasi understood its role as to protect the SED against all enemies, freeing the Party up to manage the triumph of Socialism.

The Stasi regularly grew in size. At the point of its dissolution in 1989, it maintained 93,000 professional officers and 173,000 Unofficial Collaborators (›Inoffizielle Mitarbeiter‹) or spies, referred to as IMs. These were ordinary people who spied on their colleagues, neighbours, relatives and even their own spouse.

Working under code names, they reported regularly to their contact officer, who produced monumental amounts of files, reports (containing sometimes the most banal details) and even odour samples from those deemed to be subversive. Revelation of the degree to which the Stasi watched its own people surprised even the most loyal of GDR citizens.

A surveillance technique in the exhibition

A SMALL STASI LEXICON

MfS

Ministry of State Security of the GDR, more popularly known as the ›Stasi‹.

KW

›Konspirative Wohnung‹: a safe house in which an IM and contact officer met.

HVA

›Hauptverwaltung Aufklärung‹: the Foreign Intelligence Service

OPK

›Operative Personenkontrolle‹: an Operative Person Control – collecting material about individual citizens.

IM

›Inoffizielle Mitarbeiter‹: an Unofficial Collaborator, who spied on their fellow citizens under the guidance of a contact officer.

OV

›Operativer Vorgang‹: an Operative Procedure, an investigation into the life of a GDR citizen or group.

PID

Political Ideological Diversion: any critical thought.

OibE

›Offiziere im besonderen Einsatz‹: Officers Engaged in Special Operations, working in state offices or the economy.

PUT

›Politische Untergrundtätigkeit‹: Political Underground Activity, any opposition.

Berlin, den 10.12.81

Erklärung

Ich, Alexander ~~████████~~
16.6.46
1058 Berlin ~~████████~~

erkläre mich bereit, auf freiwilliger Basis
mit dem MfS der DDR zusammenzuarbeiten.
Diese Zusammenarbeit wird inoffiziellen
Charakter tragen und bedarf deshalb der
unbedingten Einhaltung der Konspiration
gegenüber dritten Personen, Institutionen
bzw. anderer bewaffneter Organe, die
ich strikt einhalten werde.
Ich werde das MfS entsprechend meinen
Möglichkeiten unterstützen und dabei
ehrlich, objektiv und ausführlich zu den
komplexen sprechen.
Zur Aufrechterhaltung der Verbindung zum
MfS und der Konspiration werde ich den
von mir gewählten Decknamen
"Thomas Ledin" benutzen.

Alexander ~~████████~~

Pictures *Surveillance of the Blues Masses in the Erlöserkirche, Berlin 30.09.1983*

A RELATIONSHIP OF TRUST

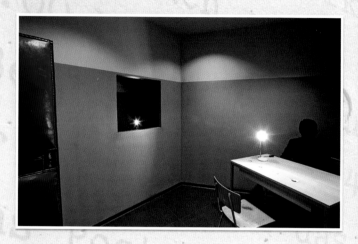

The interrogation room in the exhibition

All those falling into the hands of the Stasi underwent a different experience and yet all tell an identical story.

Having learnt their trade at a special University – the University of Applied Law – the Mfs interrogators knew what to do to extract a confession. Pulling their victim out of their everyday routine, the victim was handcuffed, bundled into a waiting car and taken off to the local remand prison. Fingerprints and an odour sample were archived and the prisoner was photographed from all angles.

Taken to his cell, the prisoner began a very long wait. With no contact with the outside world, and no lawyer, the remand prisoner perched on his stool behind a window of glass bricks. Day turned to night and still he saw no-one, read nothing and heard nothing apart from a few necessary instructions. The prisoner was relieved to go to his interrogation.

Led into a plain room with sound-isolated doors and a grill on the window, his interrogator asked him mockingly: »do you know why you are here?« After the prisoner protested his innocence, the interrogator replied, »Socialist law-enforcement doesn't make a habit of arresting innocent people.«

THE MFS IN NUMBERS

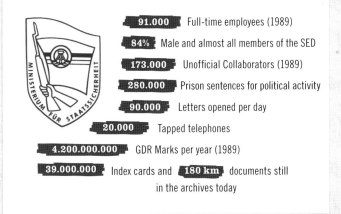

91.000 Full-time employees (1989)

84% Male and almost all members of the SED

173.000 Unofficial Collaborators (1989)

280.000 Prison sentences for political activity

90.000 Letters opened per day

20.000 Tapped telephones

4.200.000.000 GDR Marks per year (1989)

39.000.000 Index cards and **180 km** documents still in the archives today

The personal details were then recorded, twice, three times, ten times. Questions about the prisoner's private life, job, political views. Did you know about the flyers? Why do you own so much subversive literature? All interspersed with threats and insults. What do they know? What is important? The prisoner frets.

Then suddenly the interrogator is replaced. The second is much nicer. Would you like a cigarette? Coffee? It is easier to talk under such circumstances.

Oh by the way, your wife has already given a full and open confession. He throws in a few intimate details. How do they know this? Did they have a bug in the house? Have they been opening my mail? Was there a spy?

The textbook relationship of trust had been established after the third or even tenth interrogation. The Stasi man had been a good student — the prisoner tells him everything. After all, they know everything. If everybody has betrayed me, I don't need to worry about my friends. The case is passed on to the prosecution service. The Stasi operative is promoted.

»OFF TO BAUTZEN!«

The many public meetings held in that turbulent autumn of 1989 saw countless people unburdening themselves of painful experiences spanning forty years. At one of the rallies, an older man told the crowd of his imprisonment for seditious comments. In his story of harassment, maltreatment, imprisonment in a pitch black cell, hunger and forced labour, the most shocking aspect was his inability for twenty years to tell anyone – even his colleagues or family – what he had experienced.

Once he started, the words just tumbled out – it was as though a spirit had left a well-sealed grave. His speech inserted a jarring note in the atmosphere of »dialogue« and many did not want to listen. The majority of GDR citizens – even the most critical – had turned a blind eye to the terror of the early GDR.

The late years of the SED system saw the start of a practice of prisoner ransom, in which West Germany paid an average of just under 100,000 DM to purchase the freedom of around 33,700 political prisoners. The true cost of such deals was silence. The beginning of détente between the two Germanys brought clear advantages, but also meant that the victims of the SED system were often ignored in West Germany. Those released into the GDR also chose silence, as to talk would result in reincarceration. Many were unable to believe the announcement after reunification that the GDR had held some 250,000 political prisoners; but this figure has been confirmed by the documents. In the 1970s and 1980s, the GDR held more than 3,000 political prisoners at any one time. The surprising aspect of this story is the silence within the GDR on this subject during its 40 years of existence.

The most well-known prison in the GDR was Bautzen II, which housed a number of prominent dissidents and writers such as Walter Kempowski and Erich Loest, both of whom wrote books about their experiences.

The reproduction of a cell in the exhibition

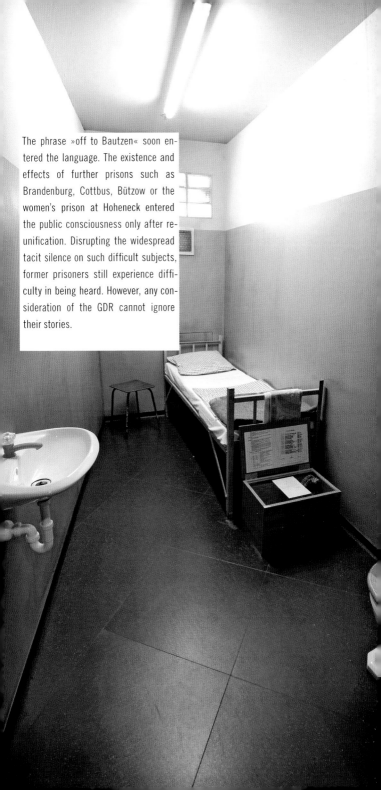

The phrase »off to Bautzen« soon entered the language. The existence and effects of further prisons such as Brandenburg, Cottbus, Bützow or the women's prison at Hoheneck entered the public consciousness only after reunification. Disrupting the widespread tacit silence on such difficult subjects, former prisoners still experience difficulty in being heard. However, any consideration of the GDR cannot ignore their stories.

THE FORBIDDEN DISTRICT

Stasi prisons were kept strictly secret. The Stasi Remand Centre in the Berlin district of Hohenschönhausen was located in a restricted area not marked on any map. Only Stasi employees lived in the surrounding streets. Prisoners never had any idea of where they were; were they to be moved from one block to another, they were driven through Berlin for hours in order to change location by a few metres. They were also taken to other institutions to receive visits from family.

▨ **Course of road not marked**
▧ **Area of the former MfS Central Remand Prison**

Pictures *The Central Remand Prison Berlin-Hohenschönhausen*

TWO PLUS TWO IS FIVE

Perhaps the last secret of the GDR is the question of sincerity: did its rulers and henchmen actually believe what they parroted or was this just a means to an end? Almost in despair, the singer Wolf Bierman asked the Party functionaries in a song: »what do you have between your ears – filth or straw? Are you really stupid, or are you just pretending?«

One thing was certain: the ideology of the SED system was not just there for show. The all-pervading Marxist-Leninism was the only legitimate world view in the GDR. Repeated ad nauseam, most schoolchildren could recite its central tenets in their sleep. The desti-

nation of history is Communism; the road to this happy goal leads through Socialism in the form existing in the GDR. Western Capitalism was currently in its death throws, and the Working Class – led by the Party – was about to overthrow it. Learnt in school, this wisdom sufficed even for doctoral exams. Although the escapist nature of these beliefs made it difficult to take them seriously, this did not prevent many from so doing.

The GDR did hold room for a great deal of hypocrisy and deviousness and even a measure of schizophrenia, but

Picture 1 May demonstration, Berlin 1953

the majority of functionaries were not mere cynics. Were the Party to announce that two plus two made five, they would believe it, ascribing it to the »higher truths« on which the Party based its pronouncements.

»Marxism is omnipotent because it is true« as Lenin taught. Such circular argumentation is irrefutable. Those not prepared to accept the ideological superiority of Marxism soon experienced its wrath. There were many channels for this anger – ranging from exclusion from education and professional training to imprisonment – all of which were very persuasive.

SED agitators did not see the point of discussions with the mistaken.

Wolf Bierman gave a clear answer to his question in his ballad to the »Truly Concerned Friend«: »They are that stupid, and act accordingly«.

THE SIMPLEST THING SO HARD TO ACHIEVE

The mural »In Praise of Communism« by Ronald Paris

When asked what they think of the wall mural, guests to the ›Restaurant Domklause‹ often say »very colourful.«

A complete depiction of the Communist utopia, the mural (finished in 1970) depicts the meagre life of capitalism, the struggle of the oppressed masses and the ascension of man into the Communist Paradise. The triptych is reminiscent of the medieval depictions of the Final Judgement. The position of Christ in this Communist salvation history is taken by a revolutionary worker. The title of the fresco was drawn from Bertolt Brecht, whose poem »In Praise of Communism« is inserted in the picture. Brecht and Ronald Paris, the artist of the fresco, both hoped that the new society would represent liberation from misery and exploitation.

The picture shows a new world of eternal sunshine. That this dream actually constituted a nightmare for so many is not shown. A just society – called Communism or anything else – remains the simplest thing so hard to achieve.

In 2010, the DDR Museum saved the painting from the condemned House of Statistics. Unveiled on 9 October 2010, its new location makes it open to the whole public for the first time.

A MIGHTY FORTRESS IS OUR GOD

The SED did everything they could to force the Church to the margins of society. Nevertheless, the Church buildings retained their impressive presence in the urban landscape, and with their doors wide open every Sunday, everyone could enter. With Church attendance on the decline, visitors to a Church entered what was to them, an entirely foreign world. People came for many reasons. Some wanted to look at the works of art, whilst many listened to the organ music. Others sought peace and quiet away from the uproar of everyday life.

Even more were searching for answers to forbidden questions. Even if sometimes unintentional, the Church represented the greatest of challenges to the state. A visible challenge to the Party's monopoly on truth, its rule ended at the Church gate.

Having had some bad experiences with the Church, the state became wise enough to avoid direct confrontation. Its attempts in 1953 to repress the »Young Church« ended in a fiasco and in the aftermath of the uprising of 17 June, the state was forced to revise its policy

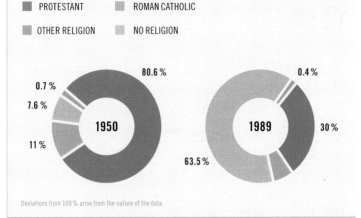

RELIGIOUS AFFILIATION IN THE GDR

■ PROTESTANT   ■ ROMAN CATHOLIC

■ OTHER RELIGION   ■ NO RELIGION

1950
- 80.6 %
- 0.7 %
- 7.6 %
- 11 %

1989
- 0.4 %
- 30 %
- 63.5 %

Deviations from 100 % arise from the nature of the data.

of expelling Christians from further and higher education. This policy was replaced by general discrimination against Christians in schools, training and the professions. The long-term success of this new policy was matched only by its perfidious nature. The death of Pastor Oskar Brüsewitz – after setting himself alight on Zeitz market place in 1976 in protest against the persecution of the Church – shifted attention to the situation of young Christians.

Unable to contain its unease any longer, the Church opened its doors to those seeking alternatives and they gathered in the Church-based environmental and peace groups and within its social work. Unhappy with the new developments, many in the Church hierarchy tried to restrain its more impulsive brethren – often with a Biblical »justification.«

Undeterred, a number of pastors and church councils protected these new groups, granting access to rooms, telephones and duplicating machines. The newsletters and flyers produced in crypts and vicarage cellars were marked »for internal Church use only«, thus legalizing their distribution.

Providing the framework for a nascent public sphere, it is impossible to overestimate the importance of the Churches in the turbulent events of late 1989. Starting with a number of small candle-bearing groups gathering in front of the Republic's many Churches, the autumn revolution came from within the Church. Peaceful protests overwhelmed the highly armed and potentially violent state apparatus.

The demolition of the St. Pauli University Church at Leipzig, 1968

GOLDEN CHAINS

Pictures *Wandlitz, 1989*

»Fat cats« muttered the people on the pavement as the large fleet of Volvos rushed past carrying the leaders of Party and State. With the entire traffic halted to allow the escorted motorcade to pass, the average GDR citizen had plenty to complain about. »So a Soviet ›Tschaika‹ is not good enough for our comrades – they need a limousine from Sweden. And we have to wait centuries for a plastic car.«

Complaints also abounded about the practice of painting the buildings flanking the regular routes travelled by these motorcades – but only as high as the passengers in the back seats could see. The houses on the side streets remained a uniform grey. Did the members of the ›Politbüro‹ actually believe that what they saw was truly representative? After all, they could have found out the reality from the Stasi reports which regularly landed on their desks. Was it these reports which they read whilst relaxing deep into the comfortable upholstery of their ministerial cars, racing across a land with which they had lost touch?

None of them ever thought to enter a restaurant in one of the side streets, to order a beer in one of the run down pubs, or survey the scanty provision in the shops. This might have boosted their popularity. Subject to total isolation, the oppressors of their fellow citizens were themselves prisoners of their own system. Secluded from real life by their bodyguards and surrounded by servile subordinates, they were united only by their mutual antagonism.

Spending their evenings in Wandlitz, the settlement in a wood just North of

Berlin was far from the opulence of the Caesars; they lived a highly unsophisticated life in modest 1950s houses. Very few made use of the swimming pool or the moderately-priced restaurant made available to them – probably afraid of meeting an enemy from the Politburo. Their wives on the other hand, enjoyed going shopping in the shops selling a number of West German products – a dream for the average GDR citizen. Many of the functionaries spent their weekends in hunting lodges, attempting to murder a few well-fed roebucks. Stasi boss Mielke had a number of antlers in his lodge. What is left of all of this? Perhaps only a verse from Wolf Biermann: *I see your gobs every morning in the papers but we will soon forget you! You swill in fat – like maggots – I will conserve you like insects in the amber of my ballads!*

»Im Neuen Deutschland finde ich
Tagtäglich eure Fressen
Und trotzdem seid ihr morgen schon
Verdorben und vergessen!
Heut sitzt ihr noch im fetten Speck
Als dicke deutsche Maden –
ich konservier Euch als Insekt
Im Bernstein der Balladen!«

Citrus fruits in the shop in the forest settlement in Wandlitz

A PLANNED ECONOMY WITHOUT A PLAN

AC 1000499

500

GDR economists were cast in the role of sorcerers. Their work resembled that of alchemists, labouring for a feudal overlord to turn base metals into gold. Some even began to suspect that their labour was in vain, based, as it had to be, on false premises. Both the feudal lords and the SED blocked their ears to such protests, ordering their minions to redouble their efforts. But the magic formula which would bring the »unity of economic and social policy« was never found.

In the 1950s, the state sought to emulate the Soviet model, concentrating on developing heavy industry. Steel works were built from scratch and whole towns emerged around them. One example was Stalinstadt, later renamed Eisenhüttenstadt. However, the new infrastructure required to serve such projects made them uncompetitive. The power stations were fed with lignite (brown coal) and after 1959 the planners embraced the refinement of Soviet oil as the great new hope for the East German economy. The magic formula was now »chemistry brings bread, prosperity and beauty«.

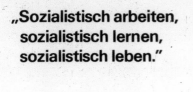

„Sozialistisch arbeiten, sozialistisch lernen, sozialistisch leben."

A new approach in the early 1960s set about reforming the structures of the economy. Less planning, greater individual responsibility and a dose of market forces were designed to bring better products. Performance-related pay was another innovation. The whole system was designated »The System of Material Leverage.« The New Economic System of Planning contained a number of good ideas, but nevertheless failed to address the problem of fixed retail prices and the rigidity of economic planning. The 1960s also saw another candidate for »saviour«, this time in the form of Science and Technology. Cybernetics was to bring the solution to all problems. As one contemporary joke ran »In 1965, the SED fed in East German economic data to a Russian computer. After much whirring of cogs, the instructions were printed: Remove the Politburo of the SED!« The problem was that the computer lacked a class standpoint. It thought in terms of logic, not Party.

With the »unity of social and economic policy« launched in the 1970s, expensive social provision diverted funds away from necessary economic and industrial investment. This crisis was compounded by the increase in the price of raw materials delivered from the Soviet Union. Falling into a chronic debt-spiral, the GDR was forced to beg for a West German guarantee for further loans. Access to foreign currency was possible only through producing competitive exports.

Grasping at straws, the SED leadership found a new panacea: the new GDR-produced 1 Megabyte memory chip.

Long held in enforced silence, in October 1989 the GDR economists were now able to tell the truth: that the GDR could only be saved at the price of cuts in social spending by up to a third, involving competitive rents, increased prices and reduced benefits. Aware that the (already hard-pressed) East German would never accept such a step, the SED chose to shut up shop.

Socialism ended in much the same manner as a company which knew it was bankrupt but sought to paper over the cracks. Those responsible fled the scene and left the problem to the liquidators.

LICENSED PRODUCTION

Western companies viewed the GDR as a land of low wages. Taking advantage of Capitalist realities, the SED allowed a number of firms to produce their goods in the GDR, thus profiting from the foreign capital which it attracted. Well-known examples include Triumph underwear, Salamander shoes, Blaupunkt car radios, Varta batteries, Nivea cream, Bärenmarke dairy products, Pepsi Cola and Kölnisch Wasser. The only condition attached to the agreements was that a proportion of the goods were to be sold in the GDR Intershop, Delikat and Exquisit chains. Unfortunately, the majority of East Germans could not afford any of these products.

BITTER NEWS FROM BITTERFELD

Passengers travelling from Thuringia to Berlin for the first time may have asked themselves why their fellow guests suddenly closed all the windows in the carriages after passing the idyllic Saaleburgen. The train was approaching the »chemical triangle« Merseburg — Halle — Bitterfeld. From the picturesque blue of the previous stop, the skies had suddenly turned a sulphurous yellow. A brutish smell pervaded. The few trees which held out bravely were covered in a white film. The semi-derelict factories littering the landscape alternated with large pyres burning poisonous material. The whole landscape resembled the most dystopian of science fiction films.

Passing a dedicated environmental law in 1970, the GDR was only the second state in Europe (after Sweden) to take such a step. The owl as a symbol of environmental protection was even a GDR invention. The reduction in Soviet oil exports at the beginning of the 1980s meant that the GDR made extensive use of brown coal, scarring vast swathes of the landscape on the hunt for this brown gold. The victim was Mother Nature: woods died, rivers were polluted and lakes were transformed into lifeless cess pits. All criticism was brushed aside by the supposed demands of economic necessity and all environmental data was classified top secret. Only the Church groups took any active notice of the environmental destruction and collecting data, they petitioned the state and sought to raise public awareness of the catastrophe unfolding in the GDR.

Particular sensation was raised by the film »Bitter News from Bitterfeld« (›Bitteres aus Bitterfeld‹). Filmed on 25 June 1988, the day of the football European Cup final, the East German environmentalists and their West German camera man all guessed (correctly) that the Police and Stasi would be too busy watching the game to notice their illegal activities. One activist remembers: »had they caught us, we would have disappeared into Bautzen for 15 years.«

The most explosive material was aired on West German television on 27 September 1988. The pictures of the »silver sea« – an open cast mine in the centre of an urban area and the waste dump »Freedom III« demonstrated the extent of the catastrophe unfolding in Bitterfeld. The widespread discussion of the film alarmed the authorities and even the central committee of the SED were worried. The events even moved East German television to counter the West German claims, and a film was commissioned praising the natural beauty of the area around Bitterfeld. Only the closure of the factories and a comprehensive clean-up programme after 1990 actually helped the region.

Picture *Diorama in the exhibition*

CHERRY JUICE AND A LEG COMPRESS

A nasty surprise early in the morning. Mandy, aged two, is running a temperature and has glassy eyes. Her entire breakfast ends up on her bib. Not an unusual problem with children of her age – the crèche is a haven for germs.

The most sensible solution would be to put her to bed with a cold calf wrap and generous amounts of sour cherry juice. However, this involves mum staying at home for which she needs a sick note from the doctor. On their way to the walk-in clinic the mother telephones her boss from a kiosk. Long-since resigned to such disruptions, he pins a notice on the door of his employee – absent due to illness. A second telephone call to the clinic is less rewarding. With the first appointment available in three months, emergencies have to endure a long wait. Appointments cannot be made over the phone. Arriving at the clinic, our two visitors are forced to register at the central reception. The 1970s and 1980s saw the state invest much time and money in modernization of the health system with increases in the numbers of medical staff.

The majority of health workers were employed in central state facilities, the larger of which were called Polyclinics and which were affiliated to a hospital. Smaller health centres were called »Ambulantoria.« Theoretically still entitled to choose freely between doctors, in reality the new system meant that the GDR citizen was allocated a doctor based on their address or that of their employer. The centralization of the healthcare system in the GDR was

Left *The company polyclinic of VEB Carl Zeiss Jena, 1983;* **Right** *Polyclinic Leipziger Str., Berlin 1974*

regarded as a key achievement. Every-thing was subject to detailed organiza-tion and all services; X rays, blood samples and EKGs was available under one roof. The patient simply took his re-cords and moved from department to department. In this way, the planners hoped to make effective use of the tech-nology available so as to compensate for the lack of trained personnel.

Mandy and mum eventually reach the Ambulatorium, a standard new building, and they join the queue at the central reception. Mandy is a little dis-tracted by the noises coming from an asthmatic Granddad in front of her. After half an hour, they have drawn a number and prepare for a long wait. Mum had hoped that Mandy would be able to sleep a little but the overheated atmosphere prevalent to all new build-ings in the GDR (windows did not open in such buildings) makes her restless and she starts crying loudly. After throwing her bottle across the room, the overworked nurse informs mum rather loudly, that she should be doing something to keep her under control. The atmosphere is stifling, a perfect breeding ground for germs – ensuring that all those not ill will soon become so. Around midday, Mandy's name is called out over the loudspeaker and she is taken to an avuncular-looking doctor. One look at the patient and he soon formulates his treatment: a cold calf wrap, generous amounts of sour cherry juice and a good sleep.

NUMBER OF EMPLOYEES IN THE HEALTHCARE SECTOR

		1970	1980	1987	1989 30.09.1989
	DOCTORS	27,255	33,894	40,516	41,544
	DENTISTS	7,349	9,709	12,527	12,802
	PHARMACISTS	2,885	3,549	4,049	4,342
	NURSES	/	98,500	103,500	/

THE ARCHIMEDEAN POINT

GDR citizens learnt the virtues of silence at an early age. If the school teacher wanted to check who had been watching Western television, she would ask how the Sand Man (a popular character on children's television) had arrived yesterday. The children smiled slyly and gave the requisite answer: »in a rocket with a red star on it«, thus showing that they had not watched the West German version. When going to national service, a father told his son: you know you are on the right path when after three months the sergeant still addresses you with »you there in the third row.«

The leading maxim in the GDR was: »what the heart doesn't see the heart cannot grieve over.« Were we to compile a dictionary of GDR expressions, it would be full of such small pearls. Fear was not provoked so much by the Stasi as by a general dread of attracting the attention of the authorities. A black mark in one's cadre file was difficult to remove.

Many people were unable, or unwilling to live such a life. Venting their anger, hate and rage in private, they returned to work only to listen in silence to the same tired old SED slogans. Others sacrificed their careers so as to maintain their self-respect. Even more tried to change the situation in their immediate environment at the cost of larger compromises. None of this amounted to true, outright opposition. Yet what options were open to the »opposition?« There were repeated individual actions involving much courage, such as the wave of protest following the invasion of Prague by the Warsaw Pact on 21 August 1968. Young people daubed slogans on the walls of houses or distributed flyers. The risk was high and the effect low. Famous artists such as Wolf Biermann managed to carve out an existence despite an occupational ban, but he was forced to depend on the assistance of others and the meagre royalties from the sale of his work in West Germany. Whatever their choice, such individuals all disappeared to the West sooner or later either voluntarily or otherwise.

Others faced a fate similar to that of Robert Havemann, who died in isolation under house arrest in a small bungalow on the edge of town.

The room for manoeuvre became greater only at the end of the 1980s. Seeking to support the peace movement in West Germany, the GDR was hardly able to praise their demands for disarmament whilst persecuting those who did so at home. Moreover, the independent peace movement was protected by its position within the Lutheran Church. They even appropriated Soviet symbolism – a muscular man recasting Swords into Ploughshares. Despite their denials, the groups constituted a political opposition. Carving out a restricted yet effective public sphere, they became the Archimedean point around which it was possible to lever out the highly armed and potentially violent regime.

1950

Protest of school children against the falsification of the elections to the GDR parliament

1953

17 June – strikes and demonstrations develop into a popular uprising

1956

Students and intellectuals campaign against Stalinism

1968

Youth protests against the suppression of the Prague Spring

1976

The writers' protest against the expulsion of Wolf Biermann

Formation of the independent peace movement »Swords into Ploughshares«

1987

Vigil for the arrested environmentalists

1989

Protests against electoral manipulation. Formation of opposition groups, demonstrations for democracy

1990

ANYONE LEFT?

The 1970s saw the development in the GDR of a new species of people: those with an application to leave the Republic, often referred to as »applicants« or »departees.« Since 1961, the physical border to West Germany had become ever-tighter, but politically easier to circumvent.

Signing a series of international agreements aimed at détente and which stipulated the freedom to travel, forced the GDR to appear more modern and open after 1972. It soon became clear that the ten or more years of imprisonment had not dampened the desire to travel latent in the GDR popula-

tion. Brandishing copies of the recent international treaties (which had been published in the GDR) a great number of its citizens went off to the interior department at the municipal council and applied to leave the GDR.

A brave step, it often marked the start of a campaign of official repression. Some were allowed to go; others were arrested and sent to prison. No few were left for years to worry about an uncertain future. In this way, the authorities hoped to deter applications. Teachers, engineers or scientists having made an application were dismissed immediately and were often lucky to

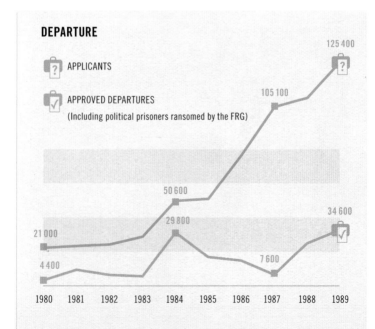

DEPARTURE

APPLICANTS

APPROVED DEPARTURES
(Including political prisoners ransomed by the FRG)

125 400

105 100

50 600

29 800

21 000

4 400

7 600

34 600

1980 1981 1982 1983 1984 1985 1986 1987 1988 1989

find even a menial job. Nevertheless whatever the nature of the state's measures, they were all counterproductive. Those subject to persecution gathered in the Church and attracted a great deal of public attention. Others placed an ›A‹ on their car which could be interpreted either as Learner (Anfänger) or Applicant (Antragsteller) or crossed out the ›D‹ and ›R‹ in DDR, leaving only ›D.‹

Even the tactic of letting such persistent individuals leave did not pay off, as every departure encouraged others to try their luck – for some, the last straw was provided by a postcard from the Mediterranean. The number of applicants rose to 250,000 by 1989. The gaping hole ripped in the iron curtain by the Hungarian decision to open her borders in the summer of 1989 prompted many GDR citizens to make off for the West. With wave after wave of East German citizens occupying the West German embassies in Prague and Budapest, it was clear that the GDR had been drawn into a profound crisis.

The Peaceful Revolution was sparked by those who had lost hope in a reformed GDR and wanted nothing more than to leave.

Such a »display of enemy symbols« could have resulted in an interrogation.

THE PEACEFUL UPRISING

The GDR turned forty on 7 October 1989, and the massed ranks of international guests and the diplomatic corps all congregated in the Palace of the Republic to celebrate its birthday.

Whilst the champagne flowed in the Parliament buildings, the general public celebrated on the Alexanderplatz with brass bands and sausages. This facade of Socialist normality covered a much more volatile reality. Those not trying to escape via Prague or Budapest stayed at home to discuss how things should best be changed. Those wishing to leave the republic via legal means marched through Leipzig shouting, »We want to go!« Many more marched to inform the world that they wanted to stay. The people had declared war on the SED.

The birthday celebrations of 7 October amounted to a wake. A large group of people on the Alexanderplatz ignored the plentiful provision of beer and sausages and at 5 o'clock they began a prearranged demonstration, demanding freedom and democracy. Filmed by the Stasi surveillance cameras, something inconceivable began to unfold: an anti-state demonstration in the heart of the capital. Waiting until Gorbachev had left for Moscow, the state now unleashed its waiting henchmen who beat back the crowds with brute force. Other cities witnessed similar violence.

The turning point came two days later in Leipzig. Overwhelmed by the sheer size of the masses, the authorities hesitated to give the order to disperse the crowds: the people had seized back power with their peaceful protest.

There was no turning back. People gathered across the republic to take a stand. Everything that followed in the ensuing months was the result of this decision to protest. A lot did follow – the wall fell, the regional Stasi outposts were occupied and the Central Stasi headquarters was stormed.

With the first democratic elections held on 18 March 1990, it was not long until the reunification of the two Germanies on 3 October. One of the most radical of revolutions was concluded within a year without a single shot being fired.

A demonstration in Rostock, 29.10.1989

CHRONOLOGY

1945

End of the Second World War. Expropriation of land owners in the Soviet zone and the nationalization of large-scale industry.

1946

Forced amalgamation of the Communist Party of Germany (KPD) and the Social Democratic Party of Germany (SPD) to form the Socialist Unity Party (SED).

1948

The Soviet blockade of West Berlin. America and Great Britain supply West Berlin by air for 11 months.

1949

7 October: foundation of the German Democratic Republic. The East German TV Company begins a test programme.

1950

First election to the GDR Parliament. Voters can accept or reject the SED-led »United List of the National Front«. The number of seats in Parliament awarded to the parties is arranged in advance.

1952

The second Party Conference of the SED announces the construction of Socialism. Prices and working norms are increased. The establishment of the People's Police in Barracks (KVP) marks the start of the militarization of East German society.

1953

17 June: strikes and demonstrations in over 700 cities and smaller towns. Soviet tanks crush the protests.

1955

First edition of »Mosaik«, the only comic book in the GDR. The first official Youth Dedication Ceremonies are performed at Easter.

1956

»Destalinization« in the Soviet Union. The Hungarian Uprising. Protests in East German universities. Establishment of the National People's Army (NVA).

1957

Show trials of critical intellectuals end with long prison sentences. The first Trabant P 50 is produced.

1958

The end of rationing. The fifth SED Party Conference announces the »Ten Commandments of Socialist Morality«. Announcement of the 60/40 directive: 60 % of music played at all concerts and other public events must have been composed and produced in the Eastern bloc.

1960

»The Socialist Spring in the Countryside« brings the collectivization of agriculture and the first crisis in the food supply.

1961

The flood of refugees to West Germany reaches its peak. The SED responds on 13 August by erecting the Berlin Wall. The order is given to open fire on those escaping. The first deaths follow.

1962

Peter Fechter is shot trying to climb the Berlin Wall and bleeds to death. National military service introduced in the GDR.

1963

The sixth SED Party Conference announces economic reforms and liberalization in cultural and youth policy.

1964

The FDJ jamboree launches a new and more open youth policy. The music and more relaxed style of the new radio station DT 64 wins a large audience.

1965

The Central Committee reverses many cultural reforms. Critical films, books and plays as well as all beat music are banned. Free access to the »planned child pill.«

1966

Ban of the DEFA-Film »Spur der Steine«. The foundation of what was to become the »Oktoberklub« leads to the emergence of the FDJ folk movement.

1968

GDR involvement in Warsaw Pact invasion of Czechoslovakia and the suppression of the »Prague Spring«. The role of the NVA is restricted to bringing up the rear.

1969

A rumour spreads that the Rolling Stones are to play a concert in the Springer house in West Berlin. Beat fans travel to East Berlin in the hope of hearing them – mingling with the crowds celebrating the twentieth anniversary of the GDR.

1970

During Willy Brandt's visit to Erfurt, the crowd breaks through the cordon to cheer underneath his hotel window. The event shows the dangers of détente for the SED.

1971

Erich Honecker succeeds Walter Ulbricht as the head of the SED. The Four Power Agreement guarantees the status of West Berlin.

1972

The Olympic Games at Munich sees the first participation by the GDR in a summer Olympics. The Basic Treaty establishes relations between the GDR and West Germany. Abortion is legalized.

1973

The tenth World Festival of Youth in East Berlin. This SED liberalizes its youth policy. Launch of the housing programme.

1974

Jürgen Sparwasser scores the winning goal against West Germany at the Football World Cup.

1976

New social measures bring young families with children a range of advantages. The expulsion of singer-songwriter Wolf Biermann sparks protest from prominent artists.

1977

Rising coffee prices leads to the development in the GDR of a replacement coffee mix for use by companies and restaurants. The retail price of coffee is raised; protests force a U-turn.

1978

The GDR cosmonaut Sigmund Jähn is the »first German in space«. Pre-military training is introduced in schools.

1981

The independent peace movement finds support for its appeal for »Peace without Weapons«.

1983

West German guarantees enable the GDR to borrow billions of Marks on the international capital markets.
The GDR removes its automatic guns on the inner-German border.

1984

The second multi-billion loan to the GDR. The GDR allows a large number of applicants to emigrate.

1986

Erich Honecker is at the height of his power at the tenth SED Party Conference, yet ever-more signs point to a mounting crisis.

1987

The GDR celebrates the 750th anniversary of the foundation of the city of Berlin. Improving the supply situation to »showcase« Berlin leads to dissent in the provinces.

1988

Civil rights activists demonstrate for freedom of speech and travel on the fringes of an official demonstration. This provokes a wave of arrests and expulsions from the GDR.

1989

East German citizens occupy the West German embassies in Budapest and Prague. Waves of refugees arrive in West Germany. Those staying in the GDR establish opposition parties. The Police use violence to disperse a demonstration on 7 October. The Leipzig »Monday Demonstration« on 9 October and those in Berlin on 4 November pass off peacefully. The Berlin Wall falls on 9 November.

1990

The dissolution of the Stasi; the first free and fair elections on 18 March; the introduction of the D-Mark on 1 July; German reunification on 3 October.

2006

The DDR Museum opens on 15 July. The permanent exhibition »Everyday life in a long-gone state« gives a hands-on experience of the history of everyday life in the GDR.

2010

The DDR Museum extends its exhibition. A range of new topics are covered over double the floor space. The DDR-Restaurant opens in the adjacent building.

FINDING YOUR WAY AROUND

1. THE BERLIN WALL
2. TRANSPORTATION
3. YOUTH
4. EDUCATION
5. WORK
6. PRODUCTS
7. CONSUMPTION
8. STATE SECURITY
9. HOUSING
10. HOME
11. FAMILY
12. MEDIA
13. FILMS
14. FASHION
15. ARTS & CULTURE
16. ACTIVITIES
17. HOLIDAYS
18. »FOGSCREEN OF THE BUREAUCRACY«
19. THE PARTY
20. FDGB
21. VOTING
22. BLOC PARTIES

DDR-RESTAURANT
DOMKLAUSE

23	MASS ORGANIZATIONS	**28**	STATE	**33**	HEALTHCARE
24	BROTHER STATES	**29**	IDEOLOGY	**34**	ENVIRONMENT
25	NVA	**30**	OPPOSITION	**35**	THE BORDER
26	INTERROGATION	**31**	THE AUTHORITIES	**36**	»IN PRAISE OF
27	PRISON	**32**	ECONOMY		COMMUNISM«

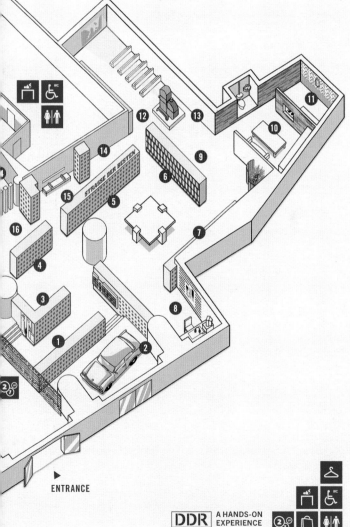

STRASSE DER BESTEN

▶ ENTRANCE

DDR museum

A HANDS-ON EXPERIENCE OF HISTORY

BIBLIOGRAPHY

pp. 25: Wolle, Stefan, Die heile Welt der Diktatur, Bonn, 1999; **pp. 36/37/38/39/46/47/51/77/131/141;** Sozialreport '90, Daten und Fakten zur sozialen Lage der DDR, Berlin, 1990; **pp. 61:** Frauenreport '90, Berlin, 1990; **pp. 65:** Die Welt 19.10.1983; **pp. 86, 87:** Statistisches Jahrbuch der Deutschen Demokratischen Republik, Berlin, 1989; **pp. 104:** Herbst, Ranke, Winkler: So funktionierte die DDR, 1994; **pp. 115:** BStU, Außenstelle Leipzig; **pp. 121:** Gieseke, Jens: Die DDR-Staatssicherheit, 2000; **pp. 144:** BStU, 1996

PHOTO CREDITS

All photographs, maps and illustrations have been taken from the archive of the DDR Museum unless otherwise stated. In a few cases, it was not possible to identify the rights holders. Should any legal claim exist, we would request that those affected contact the publisher.

pp. 14/15: Marco Bertram; **pp. 16:** BArch, Bild 183-S88622, Fotograf: Igel; Berliner Mauer-Archiv, Hagen Koch; **pp. 17:** BArch, B 145 Bild-F005191-0040A; BArch, Bild 183-U1007-017, Fotograf: Kluge, Wolfgang (detail); BArch, Bild 183-U1006-050, Fotograf: Siebahn, Manfred; **pp. 19:** BArch, Bild 183-1989-1027-023, Fotograf: Kasper, Jan Peter; BArch, Bild 183-1989-1026-031, Fotograf: Ludwig, Jürgen (detail); BArch, Bild 183-1990-0922-002, Fotograf: Gahlbeck, Friedrich; Bundesregierung, B 145 Bild-00048987, Fotograf: Seebode; **pp. 23:** Berliner Mauer-Archiv, Hagen Koch; **pp. 24/27:** Marco Bertram; **pp. 28/30/31:** Michael Richter; **pp. 32/33:** BArch, Bild 183-1984-0609-416, Fotograf: Zimmermann, Peter (detail); **pp. 32:** SAPMO-BArch, Bild Y 3 JW 408/73; Harald Hauswald; **pp. 33:** Robert-Havemann-Gesellschaft; **pp. 38:** SAPMO-BArch, Bild Y 3-JW 2019; SAPMO-BArch (detail), Bild Y 8-721-100 (detail); **pp. 39:** BArch, Bild 183-Z0116-402, Fotograf: Schaar, Helmut (detail); SAPMO-BArch, Bild Y 3-719_00 (detail); SAPMO-BArch, Bild Y 3-JW 138_81_3; **pp. 41:** Siegfried Wittenburg; **pp. 48–51:** Bezirksmuseum Marzahn-Hellersdorf; Berlinische Galerie; **pp. 52:** Bezirksmuseum Marzahn-Hellersdorf; **pp. 54/55:** BArch, Bild 183-Z0331-309, Fotograf: Link, Hubert; **pp. 68/69:** BArch, Bild 183-E0905-0034-001, Fotografin: Hochneder, Christa; **pp. 70/71:** BArch, Bild 183-L0902-114; **pp. 76/77:** Horst Laurisch; **pp. 81:** BArch, Bild 183-1986-0110-407, Fotograf: Grimm, Peer; ADN (detail); Dieter Schmidt (detail); **pp. 84/85:** Dieter Schmidt; **pp. 92:** BArch, Bild 183-S99144 (detail); SAPMO-BArch, Plak 103-008-002; **pp. 93:** BArch, Bild 183-W0910-305; SAPMO-BArch, Plak 100-014-040, Grafiker: Hujet; BArch, Bild 183-K0614-0006-003, Fotograf: Thieme, Wolfgang; **pp. 94/95:** BArch, Bild 183-M0630-101-T1, Fotograf: Spremberg, Joachim; **pp. 96:** BArch, Bild 183-1982-0821-034, Fotograf: Mittelstädt, Rainer; **pp. 97:** BArch, Bild 183-1989-0501-024, Fotograf: Mittelstaedt, Rainer; BArch, Bild 183-T0706-0039, Fotograf: Koard, Peter; BArch, Bild 183-R0522-176, Fotograf: Sturm, Horst; BArch, Bild 183-T0712-0313, Fotograf: Koard, Peter; BArch, Bild 183-K0619-0001-178, Fotograf: Koard, Peter; BArch, Bild 183-N0801-713, Fotograf: Spremberg, Joachim; **pp. 100:** SAPMO-BArch, PlakY 7/256, Gestalter: Helmut Wengler; **pp. 105:** BArch, Bild 183-1982-1014-054, Fotograf: Reiche, Hartmut (detail); **pp. 106:** BArch, Bild 183-1985-0530-032, Fotograf: Schaar, Helmut; **pp. 106/107:** BArch, Bild 183-Z0117-0005, Fotograf: Schaar, Helmut; **pp. 107:** BArch, Bild 183-82264-0003, Fotograf: Burmeister; **pp. 111:** BArch, Bild 183-R0210-369, Fotograf: Blunck (detail); **pp. 114:** Robert-Havemann-Gesellschaft / Berndt Püschel (detail); **pp. 118:** Bundesbeauftragter für die Unterlagen der Staatssicherheit der ehemaligen DDR; **pp. 125:** Stiftung Gedenkstätte Berlin-Hohenschönhausen (detail); **pp. 126/127:** BArch, Bild 183-19400-0029, Fotograf: Sturm, Horst; **pp. 129:** Münch, Sabine; **pp. 130:** Quelle: Stadtarchiv Leipzig, Geschenk Privatperson, unbekannt (detail); **pp. 132:** BArch, Bild 183-1989-1130-423, Fotograf: Link, Hubert; BArch, Bild 183-1989-1130-412, Fotograf: Link, Hubert; BArch, Bild 183-1989-1123-032, Fotograf: Zimmermann, Peter; **pp. 133:** BArch, Bild 183-1989-1130-409, Fotograf: Link, Hubert; **pp. 134:** SAPMO-BArch, Bild Y3JW 3679; **pp. 140:** BArch, Bild 183-C1012-0002-001, Fotograf: Liebers, Peter; BArch, Bild 183-N1209-0029, Fotograf: Lehmann, Thomas; **pp. 143:** BArch, Bild 183-1990-1029-014, Fotograf: Hirschberger, Ralf; BArch, Bild 183-1989-1201-046, Fotografin: Grubitzsch (geb. Raphael), Waltraud; BArch, Bild 175-L0040; BArch, Bild 183-1989-1106-023, Fotograf: Gahlbeck, Friedrich; **pp. 146:** BArch, Bild 183-1989-1029-017, Fotograf: Sindermann, Jürgen (detail); **pp. 148:** Panorama DDR (detail); Bundesregierung, 68988 (detail); BArch, B 145 Bild-F005191-0040A; **pp. 149:** Dieter Lämpe; Berliner Mauer-Archiv, Hagen Koch; **pp. 150:** Polizeihistorische Sammlung beim Polizeipräsidenten in Berlin (2117/23/24); BArch, Bild 183-F0321-0204-001, Fotograf: Franke, Klaus; Bundesbeauftragter für die Unterlagen der Staatssicherheit der ehemaligen DDR; **pp. 151:** Dieter Schmidt; **pp. 152:** Bundesregierung, B 145 Bild-00173126, Fotograf: Schaack, Lothar; **pp. 153:** Bundesregierung, B 145 Bild-00184361, Fotograf: Lehnartz, Klaus; Ines Buchmann; **all other sources** unknown (U.) / DDR Museum